BUCKETS
OF
BLESSINGS

"GIVE, AND IT SHALL BE GIVEN UNTO YOU.
 GOOD MEASURE, PRESSED DOWN,
  AND SHAKEN TOGETHER AND RUNNING OVER.
 SHALL MEN GIVE INTO YOUR BOSOM.
   FOR WITH THE SAME MEASURE THAT YE METE
    WITHAL IT SHALL BE MEASURED TO YOU
    AGAIN."
                    (LUKE 6:38)

DR. RAY BORAH

Buckets of Blessings
© 2023 by Dr. Ray Borah
ISBN: 978-1-63073-444-2

Published by:
Faithful Life Publishers
3335 Galaxy Way
North Fort Myers, FL 33903

(888) 720.0950
info@FaithfulLifePublishers.com
View on FaithfulLifePublishers.com

The ***King James Bible*** documents that *"In the beginning, God created"*—all that was or ever will be created. Every invention, every authored work, every manifestation of man-made ingenuity is simply a re-arrangement or replication of what God has created. The sage Solomon held forth that *"The fear of the Lord is the beginning of **wisdom**: And the knowledge of the holy is **understanding**"* (Prov 9:10), and further states *"The thing that hath been, it is that which shall be and that which is done is that which shall be done: and there is no new thing under the sun...."* (Eccl 1:9). This author has scrupulously attempted to provide appropriate credit when citing the work of others. Any missed citations are not by design, but uniquely his inadvertent *faux pas* for which the author accepts full responsibility. Permission is granted for the unaltered reproduction, distribution and otherwise dissemination of this authors materials with appropriate attribution.

27 26 25 24 23   1 2 3 4 5

INTRODUCTION

I highly recommend that you read "Buckets of Blessings." Why?

Read this scholarly biblically saturated explanation of God ordained generous living for YOURSELF! You will be inspired and challenged to follow the scriptural pattern for giving as it is laid out for us in the Old Testament through commandment and example, and then expanded upon in the gospels and the epistles of the New Testament. "Giving Living" is a lifestyle that produces a personal satisfaction and enthusiasm that is irreplaceable and irresistible!

Through decades of friendship and ministry as colleagues at the side of Dr. Borah I have personally observed the application of the principles found in these pages through the hands and the heart of this gracious and generous servant of God, and the joy that he exudes as a giver is remarkable. "Doc" Borah's testimony confirms that it is more blessed to give than to receive.

Read this book for the sake of OTHERS. Selfishness is disgusting, despicable, and extremely difficult to tolerate when one is forced to be in close proximity to persons of this sort. On the other hand, the recipients of both the gifts and the giver who is "hilarious" in his or her distribution of the goodness of the Lord will be encouraged and edified, and this is the perfect setting for opening someone's heart to the transforming message of the gospel and/or the principles for the maturing of the believer to Christlikeness. Godly and generous people are incredibly fun to be around. And their unexpected kindnesses opens doors for sharing Christ with others.

During the exciting years of our tenure of service together, Dr. and Mrs. Borah unselfishly dedicated themselves to the young adults of our church with focus on those who were being rescued and restored out of , stubborn, and destructive habits. As dean of the Bible college and overseeing adult discipleship, the Borah's demonstrated First Corinthians thirteen style charity that profoundly and positively attracted scores of hurting, and sometimes hardened, men and women to the Word of God and to the God of the Word.

Finally, read this book for the LORD'S SAKE. I found myself challenged over and over again as the scriptural exposition of Dr. Borah brought insight to light by the Spirit of God inspiring me to live by faith in God and His Word; trusting God to meet all of my needs, as I obey His Word. in the matter of giving. Using the sword of the Spirit, which is the Word of God, Brother Borah explores, examines, and explains a multitude of specific verses helping the reader stand stewardship and grace giving; tithes and offerings; alms-giving and lending.

How does this relate to the "Lord's sake?" "Buckets of Blessings" inspires FAITH and we are told in Hebrews 11:6, "....*without faith it is impossible to please God.*"

May I share one final verse that God used in my own personal life many years ago, prompting a conversation with Dr. Ray Borah, which led to the roots of this fine study concerning giving? It is a question asked by the Lord Jesus—*"If therefore ye have not been faithful in the unrighteous mammon* (wealth), *who will commit to your trust true riches?"* Luke 16:11.

You will be blessed by "Buckets of Blessing."

Please read this book!

— Dr. Paul Kingsbury

DEDICATION

To my Pastors, God called intrepid warriors of the faith, rightly dividing the Word of Truth *"once delivered unto the saints,"* whose legacy embraces all that is eternally true. Shepherding their flock, eschewing all the world deems commendable, they embrace earnestly the will of God for their life, and lead their people, as they are led by the Spirit of God, to endless fields of green pastures and enormous pools of still waters, where rest and refreshment abound, and peace, elusive in the world, is assured. Delivering to their people those nuggets of Holy Writ gleaned from mining God's *Eternal Wisdom* during untold hours of searching the *Scriptures,* and then weeping over truths revealed; and ever crucifying the flesh, they on a daily basis confesses their sin, concede their unworthiness as sons, and unprofitableness as servants. Known only to God are the perpetual struggles, the persistent sorrow, and the pernicious insults endured by His servant. Accompanied by that heavenly band of *"so great a cloud of witnesses;"* Abraham, Moses, David, John the Baptist, Stephen, Paul, Adoniram Judson, Hudson Taylor, George Mueller, and the list is endless, they labor not for the praise of men, for they *"desire a better country,"* an eternal city prepared by God. *"Well done thou good and faithful servant;"* their accolade will echo throughout heavens corridors as they repose reassured on the breast of their Saviour. "(*They*) have learned that there is nothing spectacular about their life, no emotional experiences to sigh after and wait upon. They pursue the plain day-to-day living the life the Lord intended (*them*) to live. This is real holiness."[1] *Selah, brethren!*

---

1 Roy Hession, The Calvary Road, Christian Literature Crusade, Fort Washington, PA, p33.

BUCKETS OF BLESSINGS

"WHEN YOU DON'T KNOW HOW TO DO WHAT YOU KNOW YOU OUGHT TO DO, GOD IS WILLING TO PUT YOUR WILL WHERE HIS WILL IS, SO YOU CAN DO IT."

Preface: ~ *"....that ye might be filled with the KNOWLEDGE of His will in all WISDOM and SPIRITUAL UNDERSTANDING...."* (Col 1:9) ix

Premise: ~ *"For with God, nothing shall be impossible."* xi

Chapter 1: ~ **Stewardship**: "Stewardship is the result of a consciousness of the reality of God's creative goodness, and of His presence in the world." ~ G. E. Thomas 1

Chapter 2: ~ **Grace Giving:** ~ "If the *Old Testament* Jew under the Law could tithe, how much more ought *New Testament* Christians under grace!" ~ R. Stedman 24

Chapter 3: ~ **Offerings:** ~ "He is no fool who gives up what he cannot keep, to gain what he cannot lose." ~ Jim Elliot 32

Chapter 4: ~ **Almsgiving:** ~ "Pray God to keep away from you the curse of a dead, unbroken *heart*." 38

Chapter 5: ~ **Lending:** ~ Boasting about an unknown future is sin. Don't count on your time. It is passing! Don't count on your career! It will soon be over. Don't count on your possessions! They will soon belong to someone else. 47

Chapter 6: ~ **Generosity:** ~ "It is not how much money I give to God, but how much of God's money I keep for myself." ~ R. G. Le Tourneau.. 56

Chapter 7: ~ **Eating the Elephant One Bite at a Time**: "*Start by doing what's necessary; then do what's possible; and suddenly you are doing the impossible ~ St Francie of Assisi*.....................61

Chapter 8: ~ **Extreme Living:** ~ "One of the secrets of life is that all that is really worth doing is what we do for others" ~ Lewis Carroll..66

About the Author..75

PREFACE

"...that ye might be filled with the knowledge of His will in all WISDOM and SPIRITUAL UNDERSTANDING..." (Col 1:9).

Everyone has an authority base on which he operates his or her life. It may be simple or complex; unconscious or well-thought-out; but everyone has one.[1] The gathering of information, to the inquisitive as well as to the indifferent mind, is the consequence of our Creator's magnificent design. *"Knowledge,"* the collection of data—truthful or not—is increased simply by living. A writer's work is created using accumulated knowledge. Exhibition of the resultant accumulation is indicative of their relationship with their Creator—God.

In 2005, a small collaborative project gave rise to the publication of three tracts on biblical principles relating to money. They were *The Ministry of Tithing*, *The Ministry of Giving*, and *The Ministry of Lending*. In 2016, an additional tract was written entitled, *The Ministry of Almsgiving*. The Lord placed numerous roadblocks in the path of this author's resolute publication efforts. It was while in pursuit of the publication of the last tract, and a reprint of the three originals, that there grew a consideration for a book—a revision/expansion of the four tracts. It was during these researching efforts that the author discovered the magnificent biblical precept of *"Grace Giving."*

"While tithing is biblical, it is not Christian. Tithing was strictly a practice, under Law, for the nation of Israel and, in the New Covenant

---

1 Ryrie, C. C. (1983). *Ryrie's Concise guide to the Bible* (p. 11). Here's Life Publishers.

of Grace, the Law has been fulfilled by Jesus Christ. Furthermore, there is no instruction or example of a *New Testament* Christian tithing. Like temples, sacrifices, dietary laws, and priests, tithing have been nailed to the cross, and no longer have an active role under the New Covenant."
~ Dale Partridge, June 17, 2019, "*Why Tithing is Biblical but it's Not Christian.*

So much for a new tract on "*Tithing.*" More on this subject is to be found in the chapter entitled "*Grace Giving.*"

The germ of inspiration the Lord planted prior to 2005, and continuing unabated through the present, has grown into a desire for further surveillance of God's *Word*, vis-à-vis a biblical perspective on finances. There is no pretension at this work being the end-all knowledge on the subject. There is, however, a desire that readers might revisit their understanding of the *Word* of God on the subject, and perhaps commit to a life of *Living in the Extreme,* which the Bible encourages.

Since "*there is no new thing under the sun*" (Eccl 1:9), why then a new book of one man's reflections? Perhaps to document a heritage, or for the preservation of a lifetime work ethic, or to define the philosophy and character of the man, or conceivably, to present his recent revelations to those in Christ.

It is the author's prayer.

"*That ye might walk worthy of the Lord unto all pleasing, being fruitful in every good work, and increasing in the knowledge of God*" (Col 1:10).

— Dr. Ray Borah
October 2023

PREMISE

"For with God, nothing shall be impossible" (Luke 1:37).

LIMITING GOD

God **Is *Not*** Limited ~ Holy, Sovereign, Immutable, Omnipotent, Omniscient, Omnipresent.

Man is a doubter…and always wants proof.

➢ God is not limited by the **Constricts Of Human Anatomy** ~ *"Behold a virgin shall conceive…"* (Isa 7:14; cf. Luke 1:10-35).

➢ God is not limited by the **Considerations Of Medical Science** ~ Luke 24:6 ~ *"He is not here…but is risen…"*

Acts 1:3 ~ *"To whom also He shewed Himself alive after His passion by many infallible proofs, being seen of them forty days, and speaking of the things pertaining to the kingdom of God."*

I Corinthians 15:3-8 ~ *For I delivered unto you first of all that which I also received, how that Christ died for our sins according to the Scriptures; And that He was buried, and that He rose again the third day according to the Scriptures: And that He was seen of Cephas, then of the twelve: After that, He was seen of above five hundred brethren at once; of whom the greater part remain unto this present, but some are fallen asleep. After that, He was seen of James, then of all the apostles. And last of all He was seen of me also, as of one born out of due time.*

> God is not limited by the **Confines Of Outer Space**

Acts 1:11 ~ *Which also said, Ye men of Galilee, why stand ye gazing up into heaven? this same Jesus, which is taken up from you into heaven, shall so come in like manner as ye have seen Him go into heaven.*

I Thessalonians 4:15-17 ~ *For this we say unto you by the Word of the Lord, that we which are alive and remain unto the coming of the Lord shall not prevent them which are asleep. For the Lord Himself shall descend from heaven with a shout, with the voice of the archangel, and with the trump of God: and the dead in Christ shall rise first: Then we which are alive and remain shall be caught up together with them in the clouds, to meet the Lord in the air: and so shall we ever be with the Lord.*

> God is not limited by man's finite **Comprehension of God's Love**. The love of God for us "… is not regulated by (my) fruitfulness but is the same at all times."[1] (John 3:16-18).

God *IS* Limited ~ "These Limitations (inabilities/impossibilities) may be said to be of three kinds: Physical, Intellectual, and Moral.

Physical "Impossibilities" ~ It is impossible for God to "*change.*"

Malachi 3:6 ~ "*For I am the Lord, I change not…*"

James 1:17 ~ *Every good gift and every perfect gift is from above, and cometh down from the Father of lights, with Whom is no variableness, neither shadow of turning.*[2]

God's Physical Impossibility may be expressed in various forms. It is not open even to God to make a part equal to the whole; to make the same thing both 'be' and 'not be' to make a 'circle' at once a 'circle' and a 'square,' or to make a 'square' out of 'two straight lines.'

Intellectual "Impossibilities" ~ God's Intellectual Inability may be represented either under the category of:

---

1 Pink, A. W. (2005). *The Nature of God* (p. 156). Bellingham, WA: Logos Bible Software.
2 With God, Οὐκἔνι: "*There is no room for*" not only the fact, but the possibility of variableness, or turning. Also (cf. Gal 3:28; Col 3:11).

Thought: It is impossible for God to conceive the false as if it were true.

Or under the category of:

Knowledge: It is impossible for God to know things that are not as if they were real things.

Moral "Impossibilities" ~ God's Moral Inability may be stated in the familiar phrases: '*It is impossible for God to lie*'" (Heb 6:18),[3] "*It is impossible for God to sin*" (James 1:13), or it is impossible for God to "*Deny Himself*" (II Tim 2:13).

The *Bible* also clearly indicates that there are a number of things that God cannot accomplish based upon ***logical necessity***.[4] For example, it is impossible for God to change (Mal 3:6; James 1:17), or to deny Himself. "*If we believe not, yet He abideth faithful: He cannot deny Himself.*" (II Tim 2:13).

The laws of logic (reason, common sense) are, once again, a reflection of God's unchanging nature. According to the *Bible*, God always acts and behaves with certain logical considerations in mind, and it is impossible for Him to do otherwise.

The *Bible* describes God as Omnipotent (All-powerful), capable of doing anything He sets out to do. God's choices, however, are always consistent with His moral and logical nature; He never sets out to do something contrary to who He is as God.

These "Divine Impossibilities" provide us with insight into God's character (holy) and power (Omnipotent), Objective (unbiased) moral truths, and transcendent (divine) laws of logic are simply a reflection of God's eternal being. They are not rulings or laws God has created, and could therefore alter recklessly, but are instead immutable (unchangeable), dependable (trustworthy) qualities of His nature

---

[3] Aked, C. F. (1913). *The Divine Drama of Job* (pp. 111–112). New York: Charles Scribner's Sons.

[4] "Logica necessity (*allows*) that a logical conclusion can be deduced from evidence provided" ~ psychologydictionary.org.

reflected in our universe. They exist because God exists, not because God created them.

➢ God Knows Not His Equal!

II Samuel 7:22 ~ *"Wherefore Thou art great, O Lord God: for there is none like Thee, neither is there any God beside Thee, according to all that we have heard with our ears."*

Isaiah 46:5 ~ *"To whom will ye liken Me, and make Me equal, And compare Me, that we may be like? (Isa 46:5).*

➢ God Knows Not A Sinner He Does Not Love!

John 3:16 ~ *"For God so loved the world, that He gave His only begotten Son, that whosoever believeth in Him should not perish, but have everlasting life."*

Romans 5:8 ~ *"But God commendeth His love toward us, in that, while we were yet sinners, Christ died for us.*

I John 4:10 ~ *"Herein is love, not that we loved God, but that He loved us, and sent His Son to be the propitiation for our sins."*

➢ God Knows Not A Better Message Than The Cross!

I Corinthians 1:17-25 ~ *"For Christ sent me not to baptize, but to preach the gospel: not with wisdom of words, lest the cross of Christ should be made of none effect. For the preaching of the cross is to them that perish foolishness; but unto us which are saved it is the power of God. For it is written, I will destroy the wisdom of the wise, and will bring to nothing the understanding of the prudent. Where is the wise? where is the scribe? where is the disputer of this world? hath not God made foolish the wisdom of this world? For after that in the wisdom of God the world by wisdom knew not God, it pleased God by the foolishness of preaching to save them that believe. For the Jews require a sign, and the Greeks seek after wisdom: But we preach Christ crucified, unto the Jews a stumblingblock, and unto the Greeks foolishness; But unto them which are called, both Jews and Greeks, Christ the power of God, and the wisdom of God. Because the foolishness of God is wiser than men; and the weakness of God is stronger than men."*

➢ God Knows Not A Better Time To Be Saved Than Now!

II Cor 6:2) ~ "(*For He saith, I have heard thee in a time accepted, and in the day of salvation have I succoured* (sic) *thee: behold, now is the accepted time; behold, now is the day of salvation."*

James 4:14 ~ "*Whereas ye know not what shall be on the morrow. For what is your life? (For) It is even a vapour, that appeareth for a little time, and then vanisheth away."*

➢ God Knows Not A Better Way To Serve Than To Be Fully Involved!

Romans 12:1-2 ~ "*I beseech you therefore, brethren, by the mercies of God, that ye present your bodies a living sacrifice, holy, acceptable unto God, which is your reasonable service. And be **not** conformed to this world: but be ye transformed by the renewing of your mind, that ye may prove what is that good, and acceptable, and perfect, will of God."*

I Corinthians 2:9 ~ "*But as it is written, Eye hath not seen, nor ear heard, neither have entered into the heart of man, the things which God hath prepared for them that love Him!"*

I Corinthians 3:9 ~ "*For we are labourers together with God: ye are God's husbandry, ye are God's building."*

CHAPTER 1

> "WHAT LIES BEHIND US AND WHAT LIES BEFORE US ARE TINY MATTERS TO WHAT LIES WITHIN US"—EMERSON.

THE MINISTRY OF STEWARDSHIP

Sadly, for many of God's children, accountability, and its consequences, are seldom, if ever, of any concern. However, the use and disbursement of those material items God's love entrusts to our care, have been given as the result of that love, and comes with the responsibility of seeking His wisdom as to their use and disbursement. Yes, "disbursement!"

The word "stewardship," whose biblical usage at times has nothing to do with material things per se, has come to be employed in both theological and ecclesiastical life as the all encompassing term for the Christian's responsibility for, and use of all things material. Even so, this general doctrinal meaning of the term does not preclude its being applied to one's body, time, talents (and) spiritual gifts or influence.[1]

STEWARDSHIP IS THE RESULT OF A CONSCIOUSNESS OF THE REALITY OF GOD'S CREATIVE GOODNESS, AND OF HIS PRESENCE IN THE WORLD

---

1 Smith, J. E. (1992). *The Major Prophets* (Isa 22:15–25). Joplin, MO: College Press.

The word "*steward*" appears only five times in the *King James Version (KJV) Old Testament* (Gen 15:2; 43:19; 44:1, 4; I Chron 28:1); and the five texts employ three different Hebrew terms. However, in Genesis 43:16 the *KJV* uses "*ruler.*" In Isaiah 22:15 the *KJV* employs "*treasurer.*" In Daniel 1:11 the *KJV* has "*prince.*" These are "technical," or "literal" uses which express no concept of stewardship as assigned by *Yahweh*. They do make clear, however, that "*the steward was one who handled the property or administered the affairs of another.*"

Isaiah 22:15–25, with its case of Shebna, makes clear that the steward was "neither ultimately authoritative, nor irreplaceable, and if he should begin to behave as if he were himself explicitly in charge, he shall be dealt with very severely."

The teaching about accountability for material things presupposes two great *Old Testament* themes, namely, 1) God's creation of all things, and 2) the goodness of the created order. With these presuppositions in mind we proceed to examine six aspects of stewardship in the *Old Testament*.[2]

In a message about Stewardship Charles Finney stated,

True Christians *consider themselves* as God's stewards. They act for Him, live for Him, transact business for Him, eat and drink for His glory, live and die to please Him. But hypocrites (*saved and unsaved*) live for themselves; account their time, their talents, their influence as their own; and dispose of them all for their own private interest, thus drowning themselves in destruction and perdition.[3]

a. Divine Ownership of All Things

Repeatedly the *Old Testament* confirms that *Yahweh* owns the earth and all creatures on the earth.

"*Whatever is under the whole heaven is Mine*" (Job 41:11b).

---

2 Garrett, J. L., Jr. Vol. 2, pp. 406–407.
3 Finney, C. G. (1839). *Sermons on important subjects.* (p. 248). London: Thomas Tegg.

"The earth is the LORD's and the fulness thereof, the world and they that dwell therein" (Psm 24:1).

"For every beast of the forest is Mine, and the cattle upon a thousand hills" (Psm 50:10).

"In His hand are the deep places of the earth: the strength of the hills is His also. The sea is His, and He made it: and His hands formed the dry land" (Psm 95:4–5).

"Thus, saith the Lord, The Heaven is My throne, and the earth is My footstool" (Isa 66:1a).

"The silver is Mine, and the gold is Mine, says the LORD of hosts" (Haggai 2:8).

Divine ownership mandates a major *quid pro quo*[4] in the human use of material things.

b. Humanity's Dominion Over the Rest of The Created Orde

Human beings were given, by God their Creator, the pleasure and responsibility of exercising dominion over the animals of the sea, in the atmosphere, and on the earth.

Genesis 1:26 ~ *"And God said, Let Us make man in Our image, after Our likeness: and let them have dominion over the fish of the sea, and over the fowl of the air, and over the cattle, and over all the earth, and over every creeping thing that creepeth upon the earth."*

Genesis 1:28 ~ *"And God blessed them, and God said unto them, Be fruitful, and multiply, and replenish the earth, and subdue it: and have dominion over the fish of the sea, and over the fowl of the air, and over every living thing that moveth upon the earth."*

Psalm 8:6–8 ~ *"Thou madest him to have dominion over the works of Thy hands; Thou hast put all things under his feet: All*

---

4 Something for something; that which a party receives (or is promised) in return for something he does, or gives, or promises ~ www.vocabulary.com.

sheep and oxen, Yea, and the beasts of the field; The fowl of the air, and the fish of the sea, And whatsoever passeth through the paths of the seas."

According to the psalmist, *Yahweh*[5] made *"man"* to be *"ruler over the works"* of *Yahweh's "hands"* (Psm 8:6). The concept of "dominion" is the possible view as to the meaning of the *imago Dei* (Image of God). That concept must be connected to one's accountability unto God. Trees and plant life were intended as food for man and animals.

Genesis 1:29-30

And God said, Behold, I have given you every herb bearing seed, which is upon the face of all the earth, and every tree, in the which is the fruit of a tree yielding seed; to you it shall be for meat. And to every beast of the earth, and to every fowl of the air, and to everything that creepeth upon the earth, wherein there is life, I have given every green herb for meat: and it was so.

However, such power was intended to be consistent with the Creator's purpose for all creatures.

David reflected on man's position as God's representative in His Creation. *"After God made Adam and Eve, He commanded them to have dominion over all the earth"* (Gen 1:28). All living creatures were to be under man. But because of sin, that dominance has never fully been realized. In fact, it was

---

[5] Exodus 3:13-15 is the first Biblical usage of the name "*Yahweh*," and we can see at the end of the passage that it is the name by which God has chosen to be remembered. The English language doesn't have an exact translation of the word "*Yahweh*," so in our *Old Testament* we see it written as "*LORD*" in all capital letters. In Jewish tradition, "*Yahweh*" is too sacred a name to utter out loud. Over time Jews started to substitute in "*Adonai*," or "*My Lord*," especially when speaking. Another common replacement is the name "*Elohim*," which simply means "*God.*" What's interesting is that these two replacement names are both used for other things as well, not just God, whereas *Yahweh* is reserved exclusively as a name for God. We see in Exodus 3:14 that God uses "*I AM*" and "*Yahweh*" interchangeably, which tells us that "*I AM*" is one way for us to translate the name "Yahweh." ~ *Biblestudytools.com.*

through a subordinate, the serpent, that man rebelled against God's order."[6]

c. **Prohibition Against Covetousness**

The Tenth Commandment of the Decalogue (*Ten Commandments*—Ex 20:17; Deut 5:2) clearly prohibited the coveting of that which belongs to one's neighbor. This is a universal safeguard against many other sins, coupled with commandments six through nine, dealing with man's relationship with his fellow man. The previous commandments (1 thru 5) deal with man's relationship to God. The Israelites were not to "long for," "desire earnestly," or "lust after" what legitimately belonged to another.

These commandments are the fundamental statements of a good and wholesome society as ordered by our Holy and Righteous God. Though believers today are not under the Law—"*What then? shall we sin, because we are not under the law, but under grace? God forbid*" (Rom 6:15). Believers, however, are under obligation to abide by the holy principles represented in the *Ten Commandments*. Nine of the Ten Commandments are repeated in the *New Testament* with added stipulations that are even greater than those in Exodus 20:3–17. The one not repeated is the command to keep the Sabbath; yet as practiced from the beginning of the early Christian church, the first day of the week is to be set aside for worship in commemoration of the Savior's resurrection.[7]

Hence, respect for property is obligatory, and violation of that respect is a breach of human accountability.

---

6 Ross, A. P. (1985). Psalms. In J. F. Walvoord & R. B. Zuck (Eds.), *The Bible Knowledge Commentary: An Exposition of the Scriptures* (Vol. 1, p. 798). Wheaton, IL: Victor Books.

7 Hannah, J. D. (1985). Exodus. In J. F. Walvoord & R. B. Zuck (Eds.), *The Bible Knowledge Commentary: An Exposition of the Scriptures* (Vol. 1, p. 140). Wheaton, IL: Victor Books.

d. Material Prosperity as Indicative of Divine Blessing and Enablement

The Israelites were said to be a people whose wealth, or material prosperity, or whose capacity to acquire such, was given by, or derived from, God.

Beware lest you say in your heart, *"…. My power and the might of mine hand have gotten me this wealth. But thou shalt remember the LORD thy God: for He it is that giveth thee power to get wealth; that He may establish His covenant which He sware unto thy fathers, as it is this day* (Deut 8:17–18).

If they obeyed the commands of *Yahweh*, numerous blessings would be given to the people of Israel.

And it shall come to pass, if thou shalt hearken diligently unto the voice of the Lord thy God, to observe and to do all His commandments which I command thee this day, that the Lord thy God will set thee on high above all nations of the earth: And all these blessings shall come on thee, and overtake thee, if thou shalt hearken unto the voice of the Lord thy God—(Deut 28:1–2ff).

Both riches and honour come of Thee, and Thou reignest over all; and in Thine hand is power and might; and in Thine hand it is to make great, and to give strength unto all. Now therefore, our God, we thank Thee, and praise Thy glorious name—(I Chron 29:12–13).

In a more personal and less collective sense, prosperity is reckoned to be God's gift: *"Every man also to whom God hath given riches and wealth, and hath given him power to eat thereof, and to take his portion, and to rejoice in his labour; this is the gift of God"* (Eccl 5:19). "When God gives any man wealth and possessions and enables him to accept his lot, to enjoy them, and to be happy in his work—these are bountiful gifts from God.

The *Old Testament* never presses what might appear to be a negative consequence to this teaching about prosperity, namely, that the poor have the disfavor of *Yahweh*. Rather *Yahweh* champions the cause of the poor.

e. **Offerings for Places of Worship**

In the *Old Testament,* the congregation of Israel made specific offerings for the construction, furnishing, or the renovation of places of worship.

And they made a proclamation through Judah and Jerusalem, to bring in to the Lord the collection that Moses the servant of God laid upon Israel in the wilderness This they shall give, everyone that passeth among them that are numbered, half a shekel after the shekel of the sanctuary: (a shekel is twenty gerahs—50 cents): an half shekel shall be the offering of the Lord. And thou shalt take the atonement money of the children of Israel, and shalt appoint it for the service of the tabernacle of the congregation; that it may be a memorial unto the children of Israel before the Lord, to make an atonement for your souls" (Ex 30:13, 16).

And as a tax.

And the king called for Jehoiada the chief, and said unto him, Why hast thou not required of the Levites to bring in out of Judah and out of Jerusalem the collection, according to the commandment of Moses the servant of the Lord, and of the congregation of Israel, for the tabernacle of witness? And they made a proclamation through Judah and Jerusalem, to bring in to the Lord the collection that Moses the servant of God laid upon Israel in the wilderness—(II Chron 24:6, 9).

And the one-third shekel

Nehemiah 10:32-33

Also we made ordinances for us, to charge ourselves yearly with the third part of a shekel for the service of the house of our God; For the shewbread, and for the continual meat offering, and for the continual burnt offering, of the sabbaths, of the new moons, for the set feasts, and for the holy things, and for the sin offerings to make an atonement for Israel, and for all the work of the house of our God.

God never condoned the burden of a loan to pay for the construction of His places of worship—He blessed His Covenant People so that their *Old Testament* tithes and offerings were more than adequate for such purposes.

f. The Tithe(s)

The evidence for the giving of tithes by ancient peoples, outside the biblical story, is extensive.

According to Henry Lansdell (1841–1919).

The picture-writings of Egypt, the cuneiform tablets of Babylonia, and early writers of Greece and Rome inform us that before the *Bible* was written, and apart therefrom, it was an almost universal practice among civilized nations for people to pay tithes to their gods; but none tell us when, or where, the practice began, or who issued the law for its observance.

During the Patriarchal Era Abraham gave to Melchizedek a tithe, or tenth, of the spoil after Abraham's military victory.

Genesis 14:20 ~ *"And blessed be the most high God, Which hath delivered thine enemies into thy hand. And he* (Abraham) *gave him tithes of all."*

And Jacob vowed at Bethel to give a tithe to God *"And this stone, which I have set for a pillar, shall be God's house: and of all that thou shalt give me I will surely give the tenth unto thee."*

Modern Protestant authors have tended to follow early Judaism by interpreting the various tithes mentioned in the Pentateuch as separate and distinct tithes. Accordingly, the "first" tithe would be the **Lord's Tithe** described in Leviticus 27:30-33.

And all the tithe of the land, whether of the seed of the land, or of the fruit of the tree, is the Lord's: it is holy unto the Lord. And if a man will at all redeem (hold back, retain possession of) *ought of his tithes, he shall add thereto the fifth part thereof. And concerning the tithe of the herd, or of the flock, even of whatsoever passeth under the rod, the tenth shall be holy unto the Lord. He shall not search whether it be good or bad, neither shall he change it: and if he change it at all, then both it and the change thereof shall be holy; it shall not be redeemed.* [8]

It included both agricultural products and animal herds randomly selected without substitution. This tithe, it seems, was to be given to, and administered by the Levites as compensation for their service in the tabernacle.

Numbers 18:8 – *"And the Lord spake unto Aaron, Behold, I also have given thee the charge of Mine heave offerings of all the hallowed things of the children of Israel; unto thee have I given them by reason of the anointing, and to thy sons, by an ordinance forever."*

18:21 – *"And, behold, I have given the children of Levi all the tenth in Israel for an inheritance, for their service which they serve, even the service of the tabernacle of the congregation."*

18:24 – *"But the tithes of the children of Israel, which they offer as an heave offering unto the Lord, I have given to the Levites to inherit therefore I have said unto them, Among the children of Israel they shall have no inheritance."*

And the Levites were expected to give a tithe of that which they received to the priests.

Numbers 18:25-29.

And the Lord spake unto Moses, saying, Thus speak unto the Levites, and say unto them, When ye take of the children of Israel the tithes which I have given you from them for your inheritance, then ye shall offer up an heave offering of it for the Lord, even

---

[8] Tithes of the land could be redeemed by paying the standard 120 percent evaluation, but tithes of animals could not be redeemed.

a tenth part of the tithe. And this your heave offering shall be reckoned unto you, as though it were the corn of the threshing-floor, and as the fulness of the winepress. Thus ye also shall offer an heave offering unto the Lord of all your tithes, which ye receive of the children of Israel; and ye shall give thereof the Lord's heave offering to Aaron the priest. Out of all your gifts ye shall offer every heave offering of the Lord, of all the best thereof, even the hallowed part thereof out of it.

A "second, or **Festival Tithe**,"

Deuteronomy 14:22-26.

Thou shalt truly tithe all the increase of thy seed, that the field bringeth forth year by year. And thou shalt eat before the Lord thy God, in the place which He shall choose to place His name there, the tithe of thy corn, of thy wine, and of thine oil, and the firstlings of thy herds and of thy flocks; that thou mayest learn to fear the Lord thy God always. And if the way be too long for thee, so that thou art not able to carry it; or if the place be too far from thee, which the Lord thy God shall choose to set His name there, when the Lord thy God hath blessed thee: Then shalt thou turn it into money, and bind up the money in thine hand, and shalt go unto the place which the Lord thy God shall choose: And thou shalt bestow that money for whatsoever thy soul lusteth after, for oxen, or for sheep, or for wine, or for strong drink, or for whatsoever thy soul desireth: and thou shalt eat there before the Lord thy God, and thou shalt rejoice, thou, and thine household....

Tithes and offerings, consisting of agricultural products and animal herds, could, because of one's distance from the temple, be converted into money which in turn could be used to buy meat and drink for use in celebration at the temple. There was also provided for eating by the donor and his family.

But unto the place which the Lord your God shall choose out of all your tribes to put His name there, even unto His habitation shall ye seek, and thither thou shalt come: And thither ye shall bring your burnt offerings, and your sacrifices, and your tithes, and heave offerings of your hand, and your vows, and your freewill offerings, and the firstlings of your herds and of your flocks: And there ye shall eat before the Lord your God, and ye shall rejoice in all that ye put your hand unto, ye and your households, wherein the Lord thy God hath blessed thee—Deuteronomy 12:5-7.

The "third tithe," a **Charity Tithe**, was to be given every third year, and put in storage for the benefit of "*Levites, the aliens, the fatherless and the widows.*"

Deuteronomy 14:28-29.

At the end of three years thou shalt bring forth all the tithe of thine increase the same year, and shalt lay it up within thy gates: And the Levite, (because he hath no part nor inheritance with thee,) and the stranger, and the fatherless, and the widow, which are within thy gates, shall come, and shall eat and be satisfied; that the Lord thy God may bless thee in all the work of thine hand which thou doest.

Deuteronomy 26:12-15.

When thou hast made an end of tithing all the tithes of thine increase the third year, which is the year of tithing, and hast given it unto the Levite, the stranger, the fatherless, and the widow, that they may eat within thy gates, and be filled; Then thou shalt say before the Lord thy God,....I have hearkened to the voice of the Lord my God and have done according to all that Thou hast commanded me....Look down from Thy holy habitation, from heaven, and bless Thy people Israel, and the land which Thou hast given us, as Thou swarest unto our fathers, a land that floweth with milk and honey.

1. The Noun οἰκονομία (*oikonomía*) and Its Cognate (Equivalent)

The English word "*stewardship*" is sometimes used to translate the Greek noun οἰκονομία—*oikonomía*, derived from οἶκος—*oikos*, "*house*" or "*household*," and "νεμεῖνη—*nemein*," "to divide, distribute, or apportion." The *KJV* uses "*stewardship*" in Luke 16:2-4, and employs "*dispensation*" in I Corinthians 9:17; Ephesians 1:10; 3:2; and Colossians 1:25.... The *KJV* evidently followed a text containing οἰκοδομία—*oikodomía* (the act of building, increasing, "*edifying*,"). Οἰκονομοί—*Oikonomoí*, "stewards," can refer to non-material reality (I Cor 4:1), "*the mysteries of God*," and οἰκονομία—*oikonomía* characteristically does.

Merrill Dennis Moore noted that Jesus "never spoke of '*tenancy*' (occupancy, tenure) as the idea in a Christian's relation to God, but always "*stewardship*.'" The teaching of the *New Testament* concerning the stewardship of material things, as shall become evident, is far more extensive than its uses of οἰκονομία.

2. Synoptic Gospels

a). *Non-parabolic Sayings*

Of importance for the stewardship of material things are various non-parabolic sayings of Jesus.

> "*But seek ye first the kingdom of God, and His righteousness; and all these things (tauta panta) shall be added unto you*" (Matt 6:33).
>
> *Lay not up for yourselves treasures upon earth, where moth and rust doth corrupt, and where thieves break through and steal: But lay up for yourselves treasures in heaven, where neither moth nor rust doth corrupt, and where thieves do not break through nor steal: For where your treasure is, there will your heart be also.* (Matt 6:19–21).
>
> Matthew 6:24; "*No man can serve two masters: for either he will hate the one and love the other; or else he will hold to the one and*

despise the other. Ye cannot serve God and mammon." (Cf. Matt 16:26a, Luke 12:15; 6:10–12, Mark 10:21b; 12:43b–44, Matt 23:23; par. Luke 11:42).

3. **Parables**

Although numerous parables of Jesus may be said to relate to the larger stewardship of life, and of the Kingdom of God (KOG), certain ones do directly relate to the stewardship of material things. In the parable of the rich fool (Luke 12:16-21) Jesus described a farmer who had accumulated such bounteous crops as to decide to build greater storage barns for future use. But, after erecting his barns, the man died. Jesus commented: "*So is he that layeth up treasure for himself and is not rich toward God*" (v. 21).

> Luke 16:1-9 has been variously identified as the parable of "*The Unjust Steward,*" the "shrewd manager" (*TEV, NIV*), "the crafty steward" (*JB*), and the "clever rogue" (*Phillips*). The manager of a rich man's affairs is dismissed, but before leaving he reduces the amount of indebtedness of the rich man's various debtors, and then is commended by the rich man for his sagacity. The parable closes with an enigmatic saying of Jesus (v. 9) "*And I say unto you, Make to yourselves friends of the mammon* (greed, treasure) *of unrighteousness; that, when ye fail, they may receive you into everlasting habitations.*" We will all have to give up our worldly goods; be prudent in time, make some real friends out of the mammon of unrighteousness; by means of that money entrusted to your care, do good to others who are in need.[9]

> The parable of the rich man and Lazarus (Luke 16:19-31) contrasts the luxurious wealth of the rich man while alive, and the concurrent poverty and ill health of the beggar Lazarus, with Lazarus's post-mortal presence with Abraham and the rich man's suffering in Hades.

---

9 Spence-Jones, H. D. M. (Ed.). (1909). *St Luke* (Vol. 2, p. 62). London; New York: Funk & Wagnalls Company.

➢ In the parable of the pounds or *"gold coins"* (Luke 19:11-27) a nobleman, who before going abroad for a time, gave to ten of his servants ten gold coins each with the instruction to trade or do business with these coins while he was absent. Upon his return he learned that one servant had made ten more coins and another five more, and these were commended and rewarded. But the third servant, who had kept the coin *"in a napkin"* and had gained nothing, was rebuked by the nobleman and had his coin given to the servant who had earned ten more coins. Jesus' climactic word was: *"For I say unto you, That unto everyone which hath shall be given; and from him that hath not, even that he hath shall be taken away from him"* (v. 26).

➢ Similarly, in the parable of the talents (Matt. 25:14-30) a master going on a journey entrusts his three servants with talents or coins, one receiving five, another two, and yet another one. The results were the same as in the parable of the pounds, except that the third servant is thrown into the darkness, or Gehenna (*the present abode of the damned, eternal damnation, eternal punishment*).

4. Acts of The Apostles

Paul, in his address to the Ephesian elders quoted, and hence preserved, the saying of Jesus, "'*It is more blessed to give than to receive*'" (Acts 20:35c, *KJV*).

5. Pauline Epistles

The Pauline teaching about the giving of money was primarily issued in the context of Paul's efforts to encourage the Gentile churches, derived from his apostolic ministry, to contribute an offering for needy Jewish Christians in Judea.

> I Corinthians 16:1-2 - *Now concerning the collection for the saints, as I have given order to the churches of Galatia, even so do ye. ² Upon the first day of the week let every one of you lay by him*

in store, as God hath prospered him, that there be no gatherings when I come.

II Corinthians 8:1-9, 15.

Moreover, brethren, we do you to wit of the grace of God bestowed on the churches of Macedonia; How that in a great trial of affliction the abundance of their joy and their deep poverty abounded unto the riches of their liberality. **For to their power, I bear record, yea, and beyond their power they were willing of themselves;** *Praying us with much intreaty that we would receive the gift and take upon us the fellowship of the ministering to the saints. And this they did, not as we hoped, but* **first gave their own selves to the Lord,** *and unto us by the will of God. Insomuch that we desired Titus, that as he had begun, so he would also finish in you the same grace also. Therefore, as ye abound in everything, in faith, and utterance, and knowledge, and in all diligence, and in your love to us,* **see that ye abound in this grace** (**Grace Giving**) *also*.

Romans 15:25-28.

But now I go unto Jerusalem to minister unto the saints. For it hath pleased them of Macedonia and Achaia to make a certain contribution for the poor saints which are at Jerusalem. It hath pleased them verily; and their debtors they are. For if the Gentiles have been made partakers of their spiritual things, their duty is also to minister unto them in carnal things. When therefore I have performed this, and have sealed to them this fruit, I will come by you into Spain.

If the Gentile Christians have received spiritual blessings from Jewish Christians, it is only right that Jewish Christians should receive material blessings from Gentile Christians (Rom 15:27), "*It hath pleased them verily; and their debtors they are. For if the Gentiles have been made partakers of their spiritual things, their duty is also to minister unto them in carnal things.*"

Christian giving

1. Should be **Motivated by *Agapē*** [10] (I Cor 13:3), "*And though I bestow all my goods to feed the poor, and though I give my body to be burned, and have not charity, it profiteth me nothing.*"

2. Should **Follow The Giving Of Oneself To Jesus Christ** (II Cor 8:5), "*And this they did, not as we hoped, but first gave their own selves to the Lord, and unto us by the will of God,*"

3. Should be **Informed and Motivated** by Christ's willing impoverishment for our sakes (II Cor 8:9), "*For ye know the grace of our Lord Jesus Christ, that, though He was rich, yet for your sakes He became poor, that ye through His poverty might be rich.*"

4. Should be **Repeated** (I Cor 16:2), "*Upon the first day of the week let every one of you lay by him in store, as God hath prospered him, that there be no gatherings when I come.*"

5. Should be **Substantial** (II Cor 8:2), "*How that in a great trial of affliction the abundance of their joy and their deep poverty abounded unto the riches of their liberality*" (cf. II Cor 9:5).

6. Should be **Done Cheerfully** (II Cor 9:7), "*Every man according as he purposeth in his heart, so let him give; not grudgingly, or of necessity: for God loveth a cheerful giver.*"

A generous sowing will yield a generous harvest of bounty, thanksgiving, and grace.

---

10 *Agape* is a Greco-Christian term referring to love, 'the highest form of love, charity' and 'the love of God for man, and of man for God.' The word is not to be confused with *philia*, brotherly love, as *philia* embraces a universal, unconditional love that transcends and persists regardless of circumstance. The noun form first occurs in the *Septuagint*, but the verb form goes as far back as Homer, translated literally as '*affection*,' as in '*greet with affection*' and '*show affection for the dead.*' Other ancient authors have used forms of the word to denote love of a spouse or family, or affection for an activity, in contrast to *Eros—Wikipedia*.

II Corinthians 9:6-15.

*But this I say, He which soweth sparingly shall reap also sparingly; and he which soweth bountifully shall reap also **bountifully**. Every man according as he purposeth in his heart, so let him give; not grudgingly, or of necessity: for God loveth a cheerful giver. And God is able to make all grace abound toward you; that ye, always having all sufficiency in all things, may abound to every good work: (As it is written, He hath dispersed abroad; He hath given to the poor: His righteousness remaineth forever. Now He that ministereth seed to the sower both minister bread for your food, and multiply your seed sown, and increase the fruits of your righteousness;) Being enriched in everything to all bountifulness, which causeth through us thanksgiving to God. For the administration of this service not only supplieth the want of the saints but is abundant also by many **thanksgivings** unto God; Whiles by the experiment of this ministration they glorify God for your professed subjection unto the gospel of Christ, and for your liberal distribution unto them, and unto all men; And by their prayer for you, which long after you for the **exceeding grace of God in you**. Thanks be unto God for His unspeakable gift.*

Moreover, "*Even so hath the Lord ordained that they which preach the gospel should live of the gospel*" (I Cor 9:14; see also Gal 6:6), even though Paul himself had not taken advantage of such support, (I Cor 9:15-18).

But I have used none of these things: neither have I written these things, that it should be so done unto me: for it were better for me to die, than that any man should make my glorying void. For though I preach the gospel, I have nothing to glory of: for necessity is laid upon me; yea, woe is unto me, if I preach not the gospel! For if I do this thing willingly, I have a reward: but if against my will, a dispensation of the gospel is committed unto me. What is my reward then? Verily that, when I preach the gospel, I may make the gospel of Christ without charge, that I abuse not my power in the gospel.

Paul's epistles contain no reference to the tithe.[11] However, his encouragement for the Christian to *"give,"* and *"give sacrificially"* is undisputed.

Promise of blessing (3:10–12).[12]

• Leviticus 25:23: *"The land is Mine."*

• Psalm 24:1: *"The earth is the Lord's."*

• Psalm 50:10: *"Every beast of the forest is Mine."*

• Haggai 2:8: *"The silver is Mine and the gold is Mine."*

• Ezekiel 18:4: *"All souls are Mine."*

I Corinthians 6:19–20: *"Ye are not your own...ye are bought with a price."*[13]

"Just as an individual is not sufficient for himself (*Shebna*—the royal steward in the reign of king Hezekiah of Judah), neither is he sufficient for others (*Eliakim*—Son of Hilkiah; the manager of Hezekiah's household.)." Depending too heavily upon human leaders is as ungodly (and unwise) as depending upon idolatry or foreign alliances)[14] The office of *"steward"* or *"keeper of the royal household"* was a position of considerable authority in Judah, modelled almost certainly on the Egyptian system familiar to us from the story of Joseph.

Shebna and *Eliakim* are mentioned together in the Biblical accounts of the traumatic events of the year 701 B.C. (Isa 36:3, 11, 22; 37:2). In all these passages, Eliakim is *"over the household"* and Shebna a *"secretary."* Isaiah's prophecy is addressed to Shebna sometime before 701, by which time Shebna had been *"thrust from his office...and cast down from his station"* as the prophet foretold (Isa 22:19).

Pharaoh appointed Shebna *"over my (Pharaoh's) house"* (Gen 41:40), and Joseph later describes his own position as *"a father to Pharaoh, and*

---

11 Garrett, J. L., Jr., Vol. 2, pp. 412–415).
12 Garrett, J. L., Jr. Vol. 2, pp. 406–411).
13 Jeremiah, D. (2001). *Giving to God: Study guide* (p. 13). Nashville, TN: Thomas Nelson Publishers.
14 Briley, T. R. (2000–). *Isaiah* (p. 226). Joplin, MO: College Press Pub.

lord of all his house, and a ruler over all the land of Egypt" (Gen 45:8). This "high steward" was the administrator of the royal estate in Egypt, a high-ranking official, occasionally even acting as regent for the king, and meriting a tomb of the most splendid quality. As well as the dozen or so references to the Hebrew equivalent of the office (e.g. I Kings 4:6; 18:3; II Kings 15:5)."

Most remarkable of all, a rock-cut tomb in the Kedron valley, dated to the time of Hezekiah, bears this inscription, unfortunately incomplete: "This is the tomb of [_____] who is over the household." Perhaps this tomb was Shebna's and, standing empty years after his death, inspired the writer of the prophecy. We can imagine the prophet pointing scornfully at the tomb: "What is the point of building yourself a tomb **here**," he cries ('*here*' is repeated three times in Isa 22:16), "*when you are destined to die in a foreign land far from* **here**?" There is no suggestion that the prophet is condemning the man for building a particularly ostentatious tomb, or that he disapproves of sumptuous rock-cut tombs in general for theological or aesthetic reasons! He is merely ridiculing the wasted effort and expense of a tomb that will never be used.

The image in Isaiah 22:17-18 seems to be that of a person picking an insect off himself, rolling it up into a ball, and throwing it as far away as he can.

Behold, the Lord will carry thee away with a mighty captivity And will surely cover thee. He will surely violently turn and toss thee like a ball Into a large country: There shalt thou die, And there the chariots of thy glory shall be the shame of thy lord's house.

A similar image appears in Jeremiah 43:12, "*And I will kindle a fire in the houses of the gods of Egypt; and he shall burn them and carry them away captives: and he shall array himself with the land of Egypt, as a shepherd putteth on his garment; and he shall go forth from thence in peace;*" and in a beautiful description, in Job 38:12–15, of dawn shaking off the creatures of the night.

Hast Thou commanded the morning since Thy days; And caused the dayspring to know his place; That it might take hold of the ends of the earth, That the wicked might be shaken out of it? It is turned as clay to the seal; And they stand as a garment. And from the wicked their light is withholden, And the high arm shall be broken.

The royal chariots and the rest of the king's possessions in his charge will share his fate. Isaiah 22:18, "*He will surely violently turn and toss thee like a ball Into a large country: There shalt thou die, And there the chariots of thy glory shall be the shame of thy lord's house.*"

The removal of Shebna, punished like the other leaders of Judah for his self-sufficiency and ill-timed rejoicing ("*for tomorrow we die,*" cf Isa 22:13), will leave room for "*my servant Eliakim the son of Hilkiah.*" "*In that day he will be clothed in Shebna's official vestments and assume responsibility for the whole weight of his 'father's house'*" (Isa 22:21-23).

This is hardly an actual prediction about a member of Hezekiah's government, but rather a prophecy about the miraculous survival of Jerusalem and the House of David during the period of office of Eliakim. In him are invested the powers and hopes of the House of David—hence the messianic interpretation of the passage.

The vestments (*robes*) are those of the priests, and signify the permanence of the appointment, as well as its religious authority, as coming from God (cf Ex 29:5-9). The "*key of the house of David*" is presumably a symbol of the peculiar authority of this official, although it is nowhere else mentioned in the *Old Testament*. The key to the gates and doors of the royal palace, including no doubt those of the armory and the treasury, gave the holder enormous power. Thus "*the key of David*" (Rev 3:7) or "*the keys of the kingdom*" (Matt 16:19) became, in the hands of Jesus Christ and His Church on earth, a telling symbol of the power to give entry into the kingdom of heaven:

O come, thou Key of David, come,
And open wide our heavenly home.

> *Make safe the way that leads on high,*
> *And close the path to misery:*
> *Rejoice! rejoice!*
> *Immanuel Shall come to thee, O Israel.*[15]

The Scarlet Letter by Nathaniel Hawthorne is a story of the controlling power of shame. Hawthorne called it a "drama of guilt and sorrow." In Puritan Boston the minister, Mr. Dimmesdale, commits adultery with Hester Prynne. She bears a child, and the community ostracizes her by sentencing her to wear for the rest of her life, a scarlet "A," for "Adulteress." Her sin is made obvious to all. But Mr. Dimmesdale conceals his sin. He keeps up an appearance of morality, but within he is tortured with guilt. After seven years he finally makes a dramatic public confession, tearing open his shirt to reveal his own scarlet "A" etched into his flesh, infinitely more painful than Hester's embroidered accusation.

No one in *The Scarlet Letter* understands redemption. No one understands that public disgrace has no benefit, and that private hypocrisy only binds us to our sins. No one in this story has hope, because no one sees how God can create beauty out of the wreckage we create. The place where sin enters in is where God Himself enters in with redeeming grace. When you read this book, you wish you could step inside it and say to Mr. Dimmesdale and Hester, and everyone there, "It doesn't have to be like this. You don't have to be controlled by shame and hypocrisy. Your past is unchangeable in fact, but beautiful in potential, because there is a Redeemer."[16] It exposes the human craving for recognition and power, and the worldly love of status symbols (*grave* and *chariots*) and the trappings of office, all of them mere husks.[17]

---

15 Sawyer, J. F. A. (1984). *Isaiah* (Vol. 1, pp. 195–196). Louisville, KY: Westminster John Knox Press.
16 Ortlund, R. C., Jr., & Hughes, R. K. (2005). *Isaiah: God saves sinners* (p. 133). Wheaton, IL: Crossway Books.
17 Kidner, F. D. (1994). Isaiah. In D. A. Carson, R. T. France, J. A. Motyer, & G. J. Wenham (Eds.), *New Bible commentary: 21st century edition* (4th ed., p. 646). Leicester, England; Downers Grove, IL: Inter-Varsity Press.

The Unfaithfulness Of The Leaders (Isa 22:15-25). Had the leaders been faithful to the Lord and called the people to repentance, there might have been hope; but too many of the leaders were like Shebna, thinking only of themselves. As treasurer (steward), Shebna was second to King Hezekiah in authority (see chaps. 36-37); but he used his authority (and possibly the king's money) to build himself a colossal tomb (22:16) and to acquire chariots (v. 18; see 2:7). Shebna was not a spiritual man, and he probably sided with the pro-Egypt party in Judah.[18]

The prophecy against Shebna is the only instance of the denunciation of an individual by name in Isaiah. In this oracle, Isaiah cited an example of the attitude expressed by Jerusalem's citizens in general.

Shebna was a foreigner—most likely an Aramean[19]—in the royal service. As steward, he was the ranking officer of the king's court. At the time of his confrontation with Isaiah, Shebna was preparing a rock sepulcher for himself. He was more interested in building lasting monuments to himself than in helping his people face the national crisis which awaited them (22:15–16). Isaiah announced that Shebna would be expelled from Judah, and that he would die in his native land.

> *Thus saith the Lord God of hosts, Go, get thee unto this treasurer, even unto Shebna, which is over the house, and say, What hast thou here? and whom hast thou here, That thou hast hewed thee out a sepulcher here, As he that heweth him out a sepulcher on high, And that graveth an habitation for himself in a rock?*

"Though the subject of Christian giving is not a doctrinal issue, it has practical values that make its study both important and profitable. In almost any conceivable type of Christian (*stewardship*), the matter of money is certain to be considered. At no other point, than in the realm of giving, do the ideals of Christian living so closely touch the mundane world in which we live. Whatever, therefore, the study of this *principle* may lack in theological content is more abundantly made up in the practical benefits received.

---

18 Wiersbe, W. W. (1996). *Be Comforted* (p. 56). Wheaton, IL: Victor Books.
19 Ancient Aramaic-speaking people inhabiting Aram (modern Syria) and part of Babylonia.

As regards Stewardship for the Christian, it is clear from an abundance of references, that the writers of *Scripture* were well aware of the importance of giving in a godly life. They certainly shared none of the mistaken ideas of many moderns who, under the guise of a superficial piety, would place money matters on a far lower spiritual plane than other doctrines, and accord it little, if any, recognition as a form of true worship.

Paul illustrates the proper importance to be accorded (*stewardship*) in his first epistle to the Corinthians. The incomparable treatise on the Resurrection found in the fifteenth chapter is unquestionably one of the most elevated and penetrating discussions of spiritual truth to be found in all the *Bible*. Yet, without a break or any semblance of an apology, the apostle concludes his discussion of the resurrection and goes on to say, "*And now concerning the collection....*" He saw no incongruity in bringing the two (*principles*) together.

But when further it is considered that the *Bible* abounds with commands, practical suggestions, warnings, and examples, all concerned with the matter of giving, the subject takes on vastly increased importance. Everywhere miserliness, greed, and avarice (*covetousness*) are denounced, and generosity, hospitality, and charity extolled. Especial note should be taken of the repeated warnings against covetousness such as Colossians 3:5, which speaks of "*covetousness which is idolatry,*" and reveals the horror of God at the root-sin of the non-giving believer, comparing it even to frightful idolatry."[20]

---

20 Stedman, *Bibliotheca Sacra, June 1950.*

CHAPTER 2
THE MINISTRY OF GRACE GIVING

Bring ye all the tithes into the storehouse, that there may be meat in Mine house, and prove Me now herewith, saith the Lord of hosts, If I will not open you the windows of heaven, and **Pour You Out A Blessing***, that there shall not be room enough to receive it. And I will* **Rebuke The Devourer** *for your sakes, and he shall not destroy the fruits of your ground; Neither shall your vine cast her fruit before the time in the field, saith the Lord of hosts* (Mal 3:11)

It is plainly evident that for Israel, the tithe was an important factor in the divinely given economy. Not only were the Levites dependent upon it for their living (in turn paying their tithes to the high priest), but much of the temple expenses (*were*) met by the tithe, and the poor and dependent of the land looked to the "Tithe-law" for succor. Under the Law, the tithe was unquestionably the divine plan for supporting and maintaining God's priests in their intercessory and sacrificial work— Ray Charles Stedman, *Bibliotheca Sacra, July 1950.*

Background Of The Tithe

The First Mention of Tithing in the Bible is in Genesis 14:20, when Abram gave tithes to Melchizidek. The Hebrew word translated "*tithe*" means "*tenth.*" When the Jews tithed, they acknowledged that

God owned everything, and that thay were grateful stewards of His wealth.

The Jews paid an annual tithe to the Lord.

And all the tithe of the land, whether of the seed of the land, or of the fruit of the tree, is the Lord's: it is holy unto the Lord. And if a man will at all redeem ought of his tithes, he shall add thereto the fifth part thereof. And concerning the tithe of the herd, or of the flock, even of whatsoever passeth under the rod, the tenth shall be holy unto the Lord. He shall not search whether it be good or bad, neither shall he change it: and if he change it at all, then both it and the change thereof shall be holy; it shall not be redeemed (Lev 27:30–33.).

As well as a tithe every third year especially for the poor.

When thou hast made an end of tithing all the tithes of thine increase the third year, which is the year of tithing, and hast given it unto the **Levite***, the* **Stranger***, the* **Fatherless***, and the* **Widow***, that they may eat within thy gates, and be filled ....—* (Deut 26:12ff).

They could also tithe on the remaining 90 percent for a special "*festive offering*" to be enjoyed in Jerusalem (Deut 12:5-19). That is a **20-30 Percent "*Tithe*" To God's Work Each Year.**

The Practice of **Tithing Predated the Law of Moses**; for not only did Abraham tithe, so did Jacob, although under dubious circumstances (Gen 28:22). For this reason, many Christians believe that God's people today should begin their giving with the tithe. A godly deacon once said, "If the *Old Testament* Jew, under the Law, could tithe, how much more ought *New Testament* Christians under grace!" The Apostle Paul outlined the *New Testament* plan for "*joyful*" giving in II Corinthians 8 and 9.

Abraham Provides Us with a Good Example of Giving. He brought his gifts to Jesus Christ in the person of Melchizidek. (See Heb 7:1–10.) We do not give to the church, the pastor, or the members of the finance committee. If our giving is a true act of worship, we will give to the Lord; and, for that reason, we should want to give our very best.

> *A son honoureth his father, and a servant his master: If then I be a father, where is mine honour? And if I be a master, where is my fear?[1] Saith the Lord of hosts unto you, O priests, that despise My name. And ye say, Wherein have we despised Thy Name? Ye offer polluted bread upon Mine altar; And ye say, Wherein have we polluted Thee? In that ye say, The table of the Lord is contemptible. And if ye offer the blind for sacrifice, is it not evil? And if ye offer the lame and sick, is it not evil? Offer it now unto thy governor; Will he be pleased with thee or accept thy person? saith the Lord of hosts* (Mal 1:6–8).

Abraham Was Prompt in His Giving. His stewardship principles were firmly fixed in his heart, so there was no reason to delay.

Abraham Was Also Proportionate in His Giving. a policy also encouraged by the Apostle Paul. (I Cor 16:1-2)

> *"Now concerning the collection for the saints, as I have given order to the churches of Galatia, even so do ye. Upon the first day of the week let every one of you lay by him in store, as God hath prospered him, that there be no gatherings when I come."*

Illustration

The pastor stood before the congregation and said, 'I have bad news, I have good news, and I have more bad news.' The congregation got quiet.

'The bad news is the church needs a new roof.'

The congregation groaned.

'The good news is we have enough money for the new roof.'

A sigh of relief was heard rippling through the gathered group.

'The bad news is it's still in your pockets.'

---

[1] *"The respect due to Me."* Fear of God does not mean being terrified of Him; it means a proper respect and reverence for Him, a reverence that leads to worship and obedience – *The Bible Knowledge Commentary.*

"IT'S NOT WHAT WE WOULD DO IF WE HAD MONEY ~ IT'S WHAT WE ARE DOING WITH WHAT WE HAVE!"

Ten percent is a good place to begin; but as the Lord blesses, we must increase that percentage if we are to practice the kind of *"grace giving"* described in II Corinthians 8 and 9.

What Was *Old Testament* Tithing?

BIBLICALLY: it was a **Command** the Jews practiced, prompted by their Love of God. *"Thou shalt truly tithe all the increase"* (Deut 14:22).

ETHICALLY: it was a **Demonstration** of an obligation the Jews had Assumed. *"Wherein have we robbed Thee? In tithes and offerings"* (Mal 3:8).

NUMERICALLY: it was one **Tenth** of the increase God had Provided. *"And of all that Thou shalt give me I will surely give the tenth unto Thee"* (Gen 28:22).

ECONOMICALLY: it was a **Surety** for the future God was Preparing.

> *Bring ye all the tithes into the storehouse, That there may be meat in Mine house, And prove Me now herewith, saith the Lord of hosts, If I will not open you the windows of heaven, And pour you out a blessing, that* **There Shall Not Be Room Enough To Receive It** *(Mal 3:10).*

Seven Certainties Concerning Grace Giving

1. Grace Giving Will Provide More Than Enough Funds For The Lord's Work—In this church age, our *Motivation* **For Giving** is not God's spiritual blessings, but God's material blessings is our ***Measurement For Giving***. There is no mandatory mathematical computation (i.e. 10%) under "grace giving." Grace giving should never be undertaken legalistically, as a chore or debt, but must be cheerfully accomplished consistently and systematically on the first day of the week. God's principle for support of the local church, and Paul's principle of giving is for, *...every one of you lay by him in store* (set monies aside for the promptings of the Holy Spirit), *as God hath prospered him"* (I Cor 16:2).

"And God is able to make all grace abound toward you; that ye, always having all sufficiency in all things, may abound to every good work (Have funds set aside to help others). (II Cor 9:8).

Lowery comments on II Corinthians 9:8

Ultimately Christians can dispense only what they have received, whether material (Acts 14:17) or spiritual (Rom 5:17). The good work is done through God's enabling.

"Being confident of this very thing, that He which hath begun a good work in you will perform it until the day of Jesus Christ" (Phil 1:6).

Regardless of how desperate one's circumstances, a person who wants to give can do so, in dependence upon God (cf. Phil 4:11–13; e.g., the widow of Zarephath, I Kings 17:9–16; and the Macedonians, II Cor 8:1–3). Once again Paul sounded the note that man's inability, by contrast, displays God's ability (Omnipotent, Omniscient, Omnipresence, etc.).

II Corinthians 4:7, *"But we have this treasure in earthen vessels, that* **The Excellency Of The Power May Be Of God**, *and not of us."*

II Corinthians 9:8, *"And God is able to make all grace abound toward you; that ye, always having all sufficiency in all things, may abound to every good work...."*

This verse is full of words indicating inclusiveness in God's enabling: **"All Grace ... In All Things At All Times, Having All That You Need ... In Every Good Work."** In the words *"all things," "all times,"* and *"all ... you need,"* the Greek heaps three words one after the other: *"panti"* "*pantote*" "*pasan*" emphasizing that **God** is indeed sufficient! His *"every"* grace "*abounds*" so that believers can **Abound** "in *every* good work."[2]

2. Grace Giving Will Enable Wise Stewardship—A fundamental axiom of the Christian life is that "whatever is withheld from God's altar may be enjoyed only for a season, and will soon become an obstruction to spiritual, mental, and physical well-being."

> *Lay not up for yourselves treasures upon earth, where moth and rust doth corrupt, and where thieves break through and steal: But lay up for yourselves treasures in heaven, where neither moth nor rust doth corrupt, and where thieves do not break through nor steal."* (Matt 6:19–20).

3. Grace Giving Will Assure What Remains Is Sufficient for Any Personal Needs—It has been said that "God will be a debtor to no man," and, "God's shovel is bigger than any bucket we have." God is the One who started the giving process—Remember Calvary?

"WHEN GOD'S WORK IS DONE IN GOD'S WAY, AND FOR GOD'S GLORY, IT WILL NOT LACK GOD'S SUPPLY" ~HUDSON TAYLOR

Failing to give is a sign.

1) we do not believe God.

2) manifests great spiritual weariness, and

3) is an indication of impending personal spiritual apostasy.

A Christian giving by grace exhibits spiritual discernment and societal discipline, and by giving exercises and enlarges his faith, which are prerequisites for remaining spiritually vibrant and financially sound.

---

2 Lowery, D. K. (1985). *II Corinthians.* In J. F. Walvoord & R. B. Zuck (Eds.), *The Bible Knowledge Commentary: An Exposition of the Scriptures* (Vol. 2, p. 575). Victor Books.

*"But my God **SHALL** supply **ALL** your need according to (**not out of**) His riches in glory, by Christ Jesus"* (Phil 4:19, emphasis added).

4. Grace Giving Will Concentrate A Focus on Spiritual Things—Those who give themselves to the Lord will be continuously active in the work of the Lord. Focused on the Savior they love, they experience no difficulty in giving their grace offerings to assist in, not as a substitute for, labor. "God sees, not the **Portion**, but the **Proportion**. If we could have given more, and did not, God notes it. If we wanted to give more, and could not, God also notes that. When we give willingly, according to what we have, we are practicing grace giving." (Warren Wiersbe).

"And this they did, not as we hoped, but first gave their own selves to the Lord, and unto us by the will of God." (II Cor 8:5)

5. Grace Giving Will Become A Catalyst for Spiritual Growth—Giving is the assurance of an eternal guarantee for remaining active in the Christian life. If all we do is receive, then we become reservoirs, with the contents falling into stagnation and uselessness. The "Use-It-Or-Lose-It" principle necessitates that we receive and disperse, thereby becoming active "conduits" for God's blessings.

"Give, and it shall be given unto you; good measure, pressed down, and shaken together, and running over, shall men give into your bosom. For with the same measure that ye mete withal it shall be measured to you again" (Luke 6:38).

AN ANCIENT ROMAN PROVERB SAYS, "WHILE WE STOP TO THINK, WE OFTEN MISS OUR OPPORTUNITY."

---

6. Grace Giving Will Create A Desire Within You to Give More—Once we know what to do, we are compelled to a consistency to do it more, and without delay.

"A man came to church with his family. As they were driving home the man was complaining about everything. He said,

'The music was too loud,' 'The sermon was too long,' 'The announcements were unclear,' 'The building was hot' and 'The people were unfriendly.' He went on and on, complaining about everything. Finally, his very observant son said, "Dad, you've got to admit it wasn't a bad show for just a dollar."

We can usually think of many excuses not to act. Dr. Bob Jones Sr. often said that "an excuse is a reason stuffed with a lie." Look for opportunities to give through your local *New Testament* church, and once the Holy Spirit presents such opportunities, act immediately.

"And this they did, not as we hoped, but first gave their own selves to the Lord, and unto us by the will of God" (II Cor 8:5).

7. Grace Giving Will Surprise You That You Did Not Start Sooner—"Giving is both the 'thermometer' and the 'thermostat' of the Christian life: It measures our 'spiritual temperature' and.... helps set it at the right level." (Warren Wiersbe) God's commands for giving are **NOT Corporate** (i.e., to the church body), but to **Individuals**. It is what we as the redeemed ones should do because we love Him. What others may neglect with ease; we should assault with vigor. *"For where your treasure is, there will your heart be also"* (Matt 6:21; Luke 12:34).[3]

---

[3] For a more in-depth study read "*Giving under Grace,*" Stedman, *Bibliotheca Sacra,* June-Aug 1950.

CHAPTER 3
THE MINISTRY OF OFFERINGS

From the Beginning: "*And the LORD had respect unto Abel and to his offering: but unto Cain and to his offering He [the LORD] had not respect*" (Gen 4:4b, 5a).

Throughout the *Bible*: God speaks directly of offerings more than six hundred times. Four chapters into the book of *Genesis* we see a major conflict erupt over acceptable and unacceptable offerings. In *Malachi*, the final book of the *Old Testament*, the focus is about offerings. In the *New Testament* the second chapter of Matthew records wise men bringing offerings unto the Christ Child. This topic, which seems to be taboo for many Christians, must be of great importance unto God. And no wonder, our Lord is King, and our offerings are our presents to our Sovereign.

Not the Tithe: When we speak of offerings, we are not addressing the issue of the tithes. The tithe was a debt owed to God; a tenth of everything that God gave to the Israelites. Notice that in *Malachi* chapters 3 and verse 8, Malachi is speaking for God when he separates the tithes from the offerings. "*Will a man rob God? Yet ye have robbed Me. But ye say, Wherein have we robbed Thee? In* **TITHES** *and* **OFFERINGS**."

"AND GOD IS ABLE TO MAKE ALL GRACE ABOUND TOWARD YOU; THAT YE, ALWAYS HAVING ALL SUFFICIENCY IN ALL THINGS, MAY ABOUND TO EVERY GOOD WORK." (II COR 9:8)

A man in a certain church made a covenant to the pastor to tithe ten percent of his income. The man was young and did not have much money. But things changed. The layman tithed one thousand dollars the year he earned ten thousand, ten thousand dollars the year he earned one-hundred thousand, and one- hundred thousand dollars the year he earned one million. But the year he earned six million dollars he just could not bring himself to write out that check for six-hundred thousand dollars to the Church. He telephoned the pastor and asked to see him. Walking into the pastor's office the man begged to be let out of the covenant, saying, 'This tithing business has to stop. It was fine when my tithe was one thousand dollars, but I just cannot afford six-hundred thousand dollars. You've got to do something, Pastor!' The pastor knelt on the floor and prayed silently for a long time. Eventually the man said, "What are you doing? Are you praying that God will let me out of the covenant to tithe?" "No," said the Pastor. "I am praying for God to reduce your income back to the level where one thousand dollars will be your tithe!" [1]

Gifts to Our King: The Hebrew word "*offerings*" means "gifts" or "presents." Chapter 1 of Malachi reveals that God was insulted and angered by the pitiful offerings brought to Him by His people. Malachi 1:6–14 deals with this issue concluding in verses 13 and 14 by saying,

> *Ye said also, Behold, what a weariness is it! And ye have snuffed at it, saith the LORD of hosts; and ye brought that which was torn, and the lame, and the sick; thus, ye brought an offering: should I accept this of your hand? saith the LORD. But cursed be the deceiver, which hath in his flock a male, and voweth, and sacrificeth unto the Lord a corrupt thing:* (Malachi ends by emphasizing God's supreme authority) *for I am a great King, saith the LORD of hosts, and My name is dreadful among the heathen.*

The *Old Testament* Jews were obligated to give both tithes and offerings. Offerings cannot begin until the **debt** of the **tithe** is paid.

---

1 Leighton Farrell, the minister of Highland Park Church in Dallas, TX.

After that, according to their ability, and God's leadership, they were instructed to bring offerings unto the Lord as a token of love, devotion, and gratitude to Him.

The Missionary Barrel Concept: Churches used to set up "missionary barrels" for the people of God to donate useful clothing for the use of their missionaries. I remember hearing of torn, outdated, and dirty items being received by servants of the Lord who rightfully felt unappreciated by those congregations. Think how God must feel when we refuse to present gifts to Him that represent value.

Offerings, Offerings and More Offerings: Freewill offerings built the tabernacle.

> Exodus 35:21: *"And they came, everyone whose heart stirred him up, and everyone whom his spirit made willing, and they brought the Lord's offering to the work of the tabernacle of the congregation, and for all his service, and for the holy garments."*

And the temple, I Chronicles 29:9: *"Then the people rejoiced, for that they offered willingly, because with perfect heart they offered willingly to the Lord: and David the king also rejoiced with great joy."*

According to *Deuteronomy* 16:16-17, every man among the children of Israel was instructed to come before the Lord, into the tabernacle or temple, three times each year to worship God with an offering. Additionally, burnt offerings, freewill offerings, heave offerings, drink offerings, etc. were all a part of the giving of the obedient Hebrew.

> *Three times in a year shall all thy males appear before the Lord thy God in the place which He shall choose; in the feast of unleavened bread, and in the feast of weeks, and in the feast of tabernacles: and they shall not appear before the Lord empty: Every man shall give as he is able,* (proportionally) *according to the blessing ("as God hast prospered") of the Lord thy God which He hath given thee.*

In the Sermon on the mount we find Christ speaking of gifts being brought unto the Lord. Matthew 5: 23a: *"Therefore if thou bring thy gift to the altar."* This is the same word found in chapter 7 and verse 11, which says, *"good gifts unto your children."* It is obvious that the second reference is not talking about tithes, and neither is the first. The use of the word *"if"* in chapter 5 reminds us that **This Giving Is Not The Payment Of A Debt To God (i.e. Tithes), But An Expression Of Our Gratitude Unto Him**.

Luke 21:1-4 tells the story of the rich people casting in great offerings unto the Lord out of their abundance, and poor widow casting two mites, out of her impoverishment, into the temple treasury. The Widow's mite was honoured above the others because of its enormous sacrifice. Similarly, as we bring offerings unto God, we are not to consider the amount given as an indication of our Lord's delight in them. Gifts that are presented at personal sacrifice resonate in the heart of our Savior, who is still observing offerings being presented at His treasury.

In Luke 21:5 we learn that gifts were used for the adorning of the temple, *"how it was adorned with goodly stones and gifts....."*

In I Corinthians 16: 1-3 we find offerings taken on the first day of the week for the needy saints in the church in Jerusalem.

> *Now concerning the collection for the saints, as I have given order to the churches of Galatia, even so do ye. Upon the first day of the week let every one of you lay by him in store* (have a cash reserve), *as God hath prospered him, that there be no gatherings when I come. And when I come, whomsoever ye shall approve by your letters, them will I send to bring your liberality unto Jerusalem.*

Acts 4:34-37 records the amazing generosity of the early church in Jerusalem as believers liquidated assets, brought the money to the house of God, and laid it at the feet of the apostles as distribution was made according to need.

> *Neither was there any among them that lacked: for as many as were possessors of lands or houses sold them and brought the prices of the things that were sold, And laid them down at the apostles' feet:*

And Distribution Was Made Unto Every Man According As He Had Need (the purpose of the offering) *And Joses, who by the apostles was surnamed Barnabas, (which is, being interpreted, The son of consolation,) a Levite, and of the country of Cyprus, Having land, sold it, and brought the money, and laid it at the apostles' feet.*

The giving of gifts by the Macedonian saints is another example of people exercising the ministry of offerings through their local churches.

II Corinthians 8:1–4.

*Moreover, brethren, we do you to wit of the grace of God bestowed on the churches of Macedonia; How that in a great trial of affliction the abundance of their joy and their deep poverty abounded unto the riches of their liberality. For to their power, I bear record, yea, and beyond their power they were willing of themselves. Praying us with much intreaty that we would receive the gift **And Take Upon Us The Fellowship Of The Ministering To The Saints***.

And who could forget the Philippian congregation's giving offerings for Paul's needs *"once and again"* (Philippians 4:15-16).

Now ye Philippians know also, that in the beginning of the gospel, when I departed from Macedonia, no church communicated with me as concerning giving and receiving, but ye only. For even in Thessalonica ye sent once and again unto my necessity."

II Corinthians 9: 7 and 8 *"Every man according as he purposeth in his heart, so let him give; not grudgingly, or of necessity: for God loveth a cheerful giver. And God is able to make all grace abound toward you; that ye, always having all sufficiency in all things, may abound to every good work."*

The Ultimate Offering for the Child of God: Offerings are gifts to God which demonstrate obedience to His command to give offerings and is an expression of our gratitude to Him for His great mercy and love to us. According to Revelation 4:11, in heaven one day, believers will lay crowns at the feet of the Lord Jesus. Our lives, our labors, our liberality in giving will be represented in these tangible rewards. "*Thou art worthy, O Lord, to receive glory and honour and power: for Thou hast created all things, and for Thy pleasure they are and were created*"

In the *Old Testament*, offerings (not tithes or loans) built the tabernacle and the temple, and funded all of God's building projects. So much was given by the Israelites that Moses asked them to stop giving. Imagine the heart trauma of God's people for a local *New Testament* pastor at having to say "Stop! Stop giving! There is more than enough money to meet the needs of the Church." *Selah*!

In the *New Testament* we see God using the local *NT* church as a place for offerings to be distributed to various needs associated with the Lord's care for His children.

Revelation 4:11 also reminds us that "*for Thou (Lord) hast created all things, and for Thy pleasure they are and were created.*" And the Lord has commanded that those items of stewardship in our possession are for distribution to the needs of others.

CHAPTER 4
THE MINISTRY OF ALMSGIVING

"But whoso hath this world's good (that by which life is sustained), *and seeth his brother have need, and shutteth up his bowels of compassion from him* (is devoid of compassion), *how dwelleth the love of God in him?"*— I John 3:17

"PRAY GOD TO KEEP AWAY FROM YOU THE CURSE OF A DEAD, UNBROKEN HEART"

NOTE: Giving to the poor is commanded by

The Laws Of God

Exodus 23:10-11

And six years thou shalt sow thy land, and shalt gather in the fruits thereof: But the seventh year thou shalt let it rest and lie still; that the poor of thy people may eat: and what they leave the beasts of the field shall eat. In like manner thou shalt deal with thy vineyard, and with thy olive yard. (cf Ex 30:15; Lev 19:10; Deut 15:7-11).

The Exhortations Of The Prophets

Daniel[1] 4:27; "*Wherefore, O king, let my counsel be acceptable unto thee, and break off thy sins by righteousness, and thine iniquities by shewing mercy to the poor, if it may be a lengthening of thy tranquility.*" (cf Jer 22:16; Amos 2:6-7).

The Teaching Of Jesus

Matthew 7:12 "*Therefore all things whatsoever ye would that men should do to you, do ye even so to them: for this is the law and the prophets.*" (cf Luke 6:36, 38; cf. 21:1–4; Gal 6:2).[2]

The conjecture of Calvin, followed by others, and mentioned early by Euthymius (377-473B.C.), that it was a practice among Jews for an ostentatious almsgiver to sound a trumpet, or cause a trumpet to be sounded before him, in public places to summon the needy, **Is Without Foundation** (Lightfoot); as is also the notion, made current by the rabbis, and accepted by Edersheim (*The Temple*, etc., 26), that by "*sounding a trumpet*" Jesus was alluding to the trumpet-like receptacles of brass in the temple treasury. There is no proof that these "*trumpets*" were found "*in the synagogues*," or "*in the streets*." "*Sound a trumpet*,".... is merely a figurative expression common to many languages, for "self-parade"—efforts to attract notice and win applause (compare our English saying about "blowing your own horn").

The contrast with the common practice instituted by Jesus is the significant thing: "*But when thou doest alms*"—"*thou*" is emphatic by its position in the Greek— "*let not thy left hand know what thy right hand doeth,*" etc., i.e. "So far from trumpeting your almsgiving before the public, do not even let it be known to yourself."

---

1 Daniel....exhort(ed) the king to renounce his sins. This points out the principle that any announced judgment may be averted if there is repentance (cf. the Book of Jonah). Daniel urged Nebuchadnezzar to turn from his sinful pride and produce fruits of righteousness (doing what is right and being kind to the oppressed)—acts which stem from a heart that is submissive to God. Had Nebuchadnezzar done so, he would have averted his seven years of insanity.

2 Hendriksen, W., & Kistemaker, S. J. (1953–2001). *Exposition of the Gospel According to Matthew* (Vol. 9, p. 320). Grand Rapids: Baker Book House.

THE REQUIREMENT OF ALMSGIVING—In the *Old Testament (OT)*, the poor were entitled to the remnants of the harvest, left purposefully in all the fields, "Handfuls of purpose" (Ruth 2:16). As well, there was the third year's tithing for "the Levite, the stranger, the fatherless, the widow."[3] "The word 'penēs,' translated 'poor' or 'destitute' does not occur elsewhere in the *New Testament*. It means 'moderate and honorable poverty,' whereas in classical Greek, 'ptocheia' implies 'disreputable pauperism and mendicancy (actively begging).'"[4]

THE BIBLE PROMISES BLESSINGS FOR THE CHRISTIAN WHO HELPS MEET THE RIGHTFUL APPEALING OF THE POOR FOR RELIEF.

Begging was unheard of in Israel until after the nation of Israel experienced captivity. Although absent from the *OT*, the word "*alms*," is found repeatedly in the (*NT*). The Hebrew word "*righteousness*," the usual equivalent for "*alms*" in the *OT*, is rendered in the *NT* "*mercifulness*," "*compassion*," especially concerning the custom of giving of alms. "*Take heed that ye do not your alms before men, to be seen of them: otherwise ye have no reward of your Father which is in heaven.*" (Matt 6:1).[5]

The "*box of righteousness,*"—Poor Box—afforded the Jews an opportunity to care for the needs of the poor, as God commanded. "*Withhold not good from them to whom it is due, when it is in the power of thine hand to do it.* (Prov 3:27) "God can bestow upon us abundantly, not only the grace which makes us rejoice in the Lord and so prepares us to give with joyful hearts (Chap. 8:2), but the grace which bestows on us that abundance of earthly blessings and that prosperity which enables

---

3 Lev 19:9-10; 23:22; Deut 15:11; 24:19; 26:2-13; Isa 58:7.
4 Spence-Jones, H. D. M. (Ed.). (1909). *II Corinthians* (p. 219). London; New York: Funk & Wagnalls Company.
5 Simon B. Parker, Ph.D.; Associate Professor of Old Testament; School of Theology; Boston University; Boston, Massachusetts.

us to give so liberally."⁶ Desiring men's praise corrupts the generosity, which is our duty to our neighbor, devotion which is our duty to God, and abstinence which is our duty to ourselves.⁷

Concern for the state of the poor is the essence of Christian duty,⁸ a duty which the early Christians did not neglect.⁹ They took care of the poor among themselves and contributed to the needs of the poor in other local *NT* churches.¹⁰. God has given us the means for meeting the needs of others; "*Let him that stole steal no more: but rather let him labour, working with his hands the thing, which is good, that he may* **have to give to him that needeth**" (emphasis added) (Eph 4:28).

The purpose of working for gain is—

1) God's plan for our temporal needs, and

2) God's provision for the poor.

"*He that giveth unto the poor shall not lack: But he that hideth his eyes shall have many a curse* (Prov 28:27)."

THE RATIONAL OF ALMSGIVING—Almsgiving became an all-important characteristic of 1ˢᵗ century local *NT* churches. Jesus and the Twelve, out of their common purse, set the pattern, and I John 3:17 demonstrates the spirit by which the Christian is energized in this duty. "*But whoso hath this world's good, and seeth his brother have need, and shutteth up his bowels of compassion from him, how dwelleth the love of God in him?*"

The duty of ministering to the saints was so obvious that there was little need to exhort the fledgling churches to assist those who were less well off, either in the local *NT* assembly or in other churches of like faith and practice. "Self-love" within the early local *NT* churches was

---

6 Lange, J. P., Schaff, P., Kling, C. F., & Wing, C. P. (2008). *A commentary on the Holy Scriptures: II Corinthians* (p. 155). Bellingham, WA: Logos Bible Software.
7 MacLaren, A. (2009). *Expositions of Holy Scripture: Matthew 1–8* (p. 220). Bellingham, WA: Logos Bible Software.
8 Luke 3:11; 6:30; Matt 6:1; Acts 9:36; 10:2-4.
9 Luke 14:13; Acts 20:35; Gal 2:10; Rom 15:25-27; I Cor 16:1-4.
10 Acts 11:29; 24:17; II Cor 9:12).

almost nonexistent (with the notable exception in Acts 5 of Ananias and Sapphira). The love of Christ and a spirit of selflessness abounded, making frequent pleas for the relief of the poor unnecessary. A laying aside for alms, in proportion to one's means, is the Biblical mandate.

The Jewish "*tithe*" is the principle of "*disproportionate giving.*" No matter one's wealth, everyone was to give the "*tithe*" = 10%. In *Grace Giving* the precise amount is "*proportionate*" and the amount is left to one's faith and love to determine—"*Every man according as he purposeth in his heart, so let him give; not grudgingly, or of necessity: for God loveth a cheerful giver*" (II Cor 9:7). Each gave freely, "*as God hath prospered* (I Cor 16:2)," and the distribution was not to the lazy, who refused to work, but to the needy.

> Acts 2:44-45: "*And all that believed were together and had all things common; And sold their possessions and goods, and parted them to all men, as every man had need.*"
>
> II Thessalonians 3:10: "*For even when we were with you, this we commanded you, that if any would not work, neither should he eat.*"

Ephesians 4:28 admonishes that we must labor to have **Sufficient To Give To The Needs Of Others**. These "*come up as a memorial before God.*" We too soon discover the futility of trying to protect earthly treasure from "*moth...rust...* (and) *thief,*" and life is often cruelly afflicted by what treasures we retain. Our desire should be to seek the permanence of heavenly treasure. Almsgiving is a way to convert earthly wealth into heavenly treasure.

THE REASSURANCE OF ALMSGIVING—Almsgiving, prayer, and fasting, are three great obligations for *NT* Christians. Almsgiving is said to be "*an odour of a sweet smell, a sacrifice acceptable, well pleasing to God*" (Phil 4:18), and "*with such sacrifices God is well pleased,*" (Heb 13:16). The Law of Moses required that the increase of the land should be equally enjoyed by "*the Levite, the stranger, the fatherless, and the* *widow"* (Deut 14:29). Then, and only then, were blessings upon one's own portion to be expected.

GOD RESPECTS NOT THE AMOUNT, BUT THE MOTIVE, PERSONAL SACRIFICE, AND THE PROPORTION THE GIFT IS REPRESENTATIVE OF THE MATERIAL POSSESSIONS OF THE GIVER.

Luke tells us that if we would make our possessions acceptable for our use, we should, "...*give alms of such things as (we) have; and, behold, all things are clean unto (us).*" The Greek phrase translated *"such things,"* is understood to mean "those possessions which are set before us, and present with us,—the earthly treasures over which God has allocated our stewardship."

See to the needs of the poor, and you can use and enjoy the abundance of the remainder. What God has declared *"clean,"* available for your use, is free from corrupt desires, and attaches no sin or guilt in its use. You may enjoy fully, such as you have. *"But.... give alms of such things as ye have; and behold, all things are clean (available for your personal use) unto you."* (Luke 11:41)[11]

THE REMISS OF ALMSGIVING—The *"righteousness"* of almsgiving does not justify a man before God. Romans chapters 3-5 prove such claims baseless. Our alms-deeds do not guarantee heaven, but it is pure religion.

> *"Pure religion and undefiled before God and the Father is this, To visit the fatherless and widows in their affliction, and to keep himself unspotted from the world"* (James 1:27)

And will be a test at the *Judgment Seat of Christ.*

---

11 *Strong's Notes, Online Bible* Electronic edition.

II Corinthians 5:10: "*For we must all appear before the judgment seat of Christ; that everyone may receive the things done in his body, according to that he hath done, whether it be good or bad.*"

To the Jew also, there were three cardinal works of the religious life; three great pillars on which they established the good life—*almsgiving*, *prayer*, and *fasting*. Jesus did not dispute these teachings for a moment, but what troubled Him was that so often the wrong motives detract from the finest methods.

A Man May *Pray*, without addressing his prayers to God, but focusing them to garner the accolades of his fellow man. If his prayers flaunt his piety, he may gain the reputation of being a devout man—**but that is all he will ever receive.**

A Man May *Fast*, so that all men know he is fasting. He will appear self-disciplined and moderate in appetite—**but recognition is all he will ever receive.**

A Man May *Give Alms From a Sense of Duty*, because he feels that giving is a duty, which he cannot escape—**but a sense of personal relief is all that he will receive.**

A Man May *Give Alms* from *a Motive of Prestige*, to demonstrate his own generosity, and bask in the warmth of the gratitude and praise of men. We are not to avoid publicity, but that "*spirit*" which "*desires*" publicity. "The true Christian cares not how much man hears of his *public* charities, or how little they hear of his *private* ones."[12]

A Man May *Give Alms* **Simply** *Because He Must*. Try as he may, he cannot rid himself of a sense of responsibility for the man in need.

A rabbinic tradition lists several types of almsgivers:

1) "He that has a mind to give..."
2) "He that has a mind to give, but not that others should give. He begrudges what belongs to others."

---

12 Attributed to Augustus Toplady (1740-1778. Source unknown

3) "He that has a mind that others should give, but not that he should give. He begrudges what belongs to himself."

4) "He that has a mind not to give himself, and those others should not give. He is a wicked man."

5) "He that has a mind to give, and those others should give. He is a saintly man"[13]

"THOSE WHO HAVE GOD FOR THEIR INHERITANCE, AND THEIR PORTION FOREVER, OUGHT TO LOOK WITH HOLY CONTEMPT AND INDIFFERENCE UPON THE POSSESSIONS OF THIS WORLD."

THE REWARD OF ALMSGIVING—We must give to others as Jesus Christ gave Himself to us, through the inherent outpouring of a loving heart. What is given to the poor, or done for them, God will consider as being lent to Him, "*lent upon interest*," the *Word* of God so signifies, and God will be a debtor to no man. "*He that hath pity upon the poor lendeth unto the LORD; and that which he hath given will He* (the LORD) *pay him* (the giver) *again*" (Prov 19:17).

Almsgiving Sends Supply of Temporal Things—"*There is that scattereth, and yet increaseth; and there is that withholdeth more than is meet, but it tendeth to poverty*" (Prov 11:24).

Almsgiving Solidifies Security from Want—"*He that giveth unto the poor shall not lack but he that hideth his eyes shall have many a curse*" (Prov 28:27).

Almsgiving Supplies Succor in Distress—"*Blessed is he that considereth the poor: the LORD will deliver him (the giver) in time of trouble*" (Psm 41:1).

Almsgiving Strengthens Sacred Honor and a Good Name—The man that feareth the Lord "*...hath dispersed, he hath given to the poor; his*

---

13 Matthew Henry, E4's *Matthew Henry's Concise Commentary* (electronic ed.)

righteousness endureth forever; his horn shall be exalted with honour" (Psm 112:9).

Almsgiving Secures Surprising Riches—*"But when thou makest a feast, call the poor, the maimed, the lame, the blind: And thou shalt be blessed; for they cannot recompense thee: for thou shalt be recompensed at the resurrection of the just"* (Luke 14:13-14).[14]

JESUS' COMMAND CONTAINS NO CONDITIONAL "IF" ABOUT GIVING MONEY TO THE NEEDY

Almsgiving Is Mandatory. Although Jesus warned against performing acts of righteousness publicly for human praise, He did not mean that such acts of generosity were optional. In II Corinthians 9:9, Paul resorts to *Scripture* to make his point. *"He hath dispersed, he hath given to the poor; his righteousness endureth forever; his horn shall be exalted with honour,* "i.e., God will remember his sacrifices forever.

The Greek word *"poor"* meaning *"one who is destitute,"* only appears here in the *NT*. The Greco-Roman culture assumed that it was pointless to give anything to a pauper. The only repayment he could make was with his praise, which they considered worthless. The biblical concern for those in wretched poverty differs markedly from this view.[15] Showing benevolence to the poor and needy was a sign of righteousness in the *OT and* is Commanded in the *NT*. Man's obedience in the matter of almsgiving obligates God to provide His Presence, His promise, His protection, His provision, and His peace to that man. Why do we hesitate to comply?

---

14 Sproul, R. (1996, c1991). *Following Christ.* Wheaton, IL: Tyndale House Publishers, Electronic edition
15 Richardson, K. A. (2001, c1997). Vol. 36: James (electronic ed.). Logos Library System; *The New American Commentary*. Nashville: Broadman & Holman Publishers. 125

Chapter 5
THE MINISTRY OF LENDING

A spiritual "*vision*" is produced by the Holy Spirit in the hearts of consecrated people, living sacrificially in the perfect will of God as faithful stewards of God's provision. However, such a person can be wrong in spiritual matters and bring devastating consequences, as in the case of the ten spies counseling not to enter the Promised Land.

The tendency of a person to be wrong comes from the reality that God's ways are opposite those of man's natural inclinations. Just as there is the tendency for the majority to follow natural preferences, so there is the danger of a few hindering what God wants to do through the majority. Thus, a divided vote is a signal to stop with the matter and search out the spiritual condition and perception of those making the decision.

In the phrase "*ye that say.*" (James 4:13) James is asking, in effect: How can you, being the kind of creature that you are, presume to dictate the course of future events? The fragility of human life, and the consequent uncertainty of all human plans, is the main point of the verse.[1]

In the case of financial obligations in the church, even though the will of the majority would be to borrow money, there may be those within the church who have a deep sense that this is a form of unbelief, which *Scripture* is so clear in warning against. These individuals may not vocally object, but their mental reservations and lack of enthusiasm will affect the spirit of fellowship within the church.

---

1 Moo, D. J. (2000). *The Letter of James* (pp. 202–203). Grand Rapids, MI; Leicester, England: Eerdmans; Apollos.

As the following verses make clear, James is not rebuking these merchants for their plans or even for their desire to make a profit. He rebukes them rather for the "this-worldly self-confidence" they exhibit in pursuing these goals—a danger, it must be said, to which businesspeople are particularly susceptible.

And we should guard here against another kind of misinterpretation: the idea that James is forbidding Christians from all forms of planning or of concern for the future. Taking out life insurance and saving for retirement, for instance, may very well be a form of wise stewardship. What James rebukes here, is clear, "*But now ye rejoice in your boastings: all such rejoicing is evil. Therefore to him that knoweth to do good, and doeth it not, to him it is sin*" (James 4:16-17). Any kind of planning for the future stemming from overconfidence in our ability to determine the course of future events is mistaken.[2]

This section gives another example of the "*wisdom*" that characterizes the world "*For that ye ought to say, If the Lord will, we shall live, and do this, or that*" (James 4:15). James addresses businessmen, probably Christians, since v. 16 seems to suggest that the readers know that their practice is wrong. "The key to avoiding boasting is to maintain a godly perspective"[3] "*For that ye ought to say*" is a pointed call for attention that indicates the seriousness of what follows. The present tense (λέγοντες—*legontes*, "*say*"—continually saying) implies that the situation under consideration was not an isolated instance. It was something that occurred frequently.

Business travel in the first century was common, and Jews traveled widely for business purposes. *New Testament* examples are Aquila and Priscilla (Acts 18:2, 18; Rom 16:3) and Lydia (Acts 16:14). Notice the well-laid plan: (1) "*go to this or that city*," (2) "*spend a year there*," (3) "*carry on business*." and (4) "*make money*." The starting time is arranged—"*today or tomorrow*." The city has been selected—the Greek text simply says, "*this city*." But God has no place in their plans.

---

2 Moo, D. J., 203).
3 Blue, J. R. (1985). *James*. In J. F. Walvoord & R. B. Zuck (Eds.), *The Bible Knowledge Commentary: An Exposition of the Scriptures* (Vol. 2, p. 831). Victor Books.

History Of Lending In The Bible

In the Jewish economy, borrowing and lending are taken for granted as existing, but the Hebrew creditor is required to release his Hebrew brother as debtor in the 7th year, though he may exact payment from a foreigner.

In Exodus 22:25, lending on interest to the poor is prohibited.
~ *"If thou lend money to any of my people that is poor by thee, thou shalt not be to him as an usurer, neither shalt thou lay upon him usury."*

Deuteronomy 23:19-20

Thou shalt not lend upon usury to thy brother; usury of money, usury of victuals, usury of anything that is lent upon usury: Unto a stranger thou mayest lend upon usury; but unto thy brother thou shalt not lend upon usury: that the Lord thy God may bless thee in all that thou settest thine hand to in the land whither thou goest to possess it.

~ Israel may lend, and will be able to lend, because of *Yahweh's* blessing, to other nations, but Israel must not borrow from other nations.

~ A pledge, or security, must not be taken in person by the creditor from the house of the debtor, nor kept overnight, if the debtor be poor.

In Leviticus 25:35-38, because of the goodness of *Yahweh* to Israel, the Israelites may receive no interest from his poor brother.

And if thy brother be waxen poor and fallen in decay with thee; then thou shalt relieve him: yea, though he be a stranger, or a sojourner; that he may live with thee. Take thou no usury of him, or increase: but fear thy God; that thy brother may live with thee. Thou shalt not give him thy money upon usury, nor lend him thy victuals for increase. I am the Lord your God, Which brought you forth out of the land of Egypt, to give you the land of Canaan, and to be your God.

Notwithstanding the prohibition of the early laws against lending on interest or usury, the same seems to have become common in Israel before the exile (Isa 24:2; Jer 15:10), was practiced on the return, and was an evil which Nehemiah corrected.

> *Then I consulted with myself, and I rebuked the nobles, and the rulers, and said unto them, Ye exact usury, every one of his brother. And I set a great assembly against them. And I said unto them, We after our ability have redeemed our brethren the Jews, which were sold unto the heathen; and will ye even sell your brethren? or shall they be sold unto us? Then held they their peace and found nothing to answer. Also I said, It is not good that ye do: ought ye not to walk in the fear of our God because of the reproach of the heathen our enemies? I, likewise, and my brethren, and my servants, might exact of them money and corn: I pray you, let us leave off this usury.* (Neh 5:7-10).

Lending to the needy was regarded as a mark of a pious Hebrew, but no interest was to be charged.

Psalms 37:26, "*He is ever merciful, and lendeth; And his seed is blessed.*"

Psalm 112:5, "*A good man sheweth favour, and lendeth: He will guide his affairs with discretion.*"

Proverbs 19:17, "*He that hath pity upon the poor lendeth unto the Lord; And that which he hath given will He pay him again.*"

Jesus teaches that His followers should lend, even to enemies, to men from whom they have no reasonable hope of expecting anything in return, because thus to do is to be like the Most High.

> *And if ye lend to them of whom ye hope to receive, what thank have ye? for sinners also lend to sinners, to receive as much again. But love ye your enemies, and do good, and lend, hoping for nothing again; and your reward shall be great, and ye shall be the children of the Highest: for He is kind unto the unthankful and to the evil*—(Luke 6:34-35).

> "*Whereas ye know not what shall be on the morrow. For what is your life? It is even a vapour, that appeareth for a little time, and then vanisheth away*"—(James 4:14)

No allowance is made for unforeseen circumstances. These businessmen are confident that they will be able to carry their plans through to completion. And so, James points out their fallacy. They "do not even know what will happen tomorrow," to say nothing about a year from now. They have been planning as if they know exactly what the future holds, or even as if they have control of the future. Not only is their knowledge limited, but their very lives are uncertain. They may not be here next year. A point of significant consequence for present day Christians individually, or collectively in their local *NT* church, to heed in all their fiscal considerations.

To point up the transitory nature of life, James employs another illustration from nature—"*Life is even a vapour.*" James borrowed that figure from the book of Job where you find many pictures of the brevity of life. In the morning, a mist covers the countryside; before noon it is gone. But some of James's readers had been planning as if they were going to be here forever![4]

However, "*My days are swifter than a weaver's shuttle*" (Job 7:6).

"*The cloud is consumed and vanisheth away*" (Job 7:9).

"*Our days upon earth are a shadow*" (Job 8:9).

"*Now(the passing of) my days are swifter than a post*" (Job 9:25)

Referring to the royal couriers that hastened in their missions. "*They are passed away as the swift ships: as the eagle that hasteth to the prey*" (Job 9:26).

---

[4] Burdick, D. W. (1981). *James*. In F. E. Gaebelein (Ed.), *The Expositor's Bible Commentary: Hebrews through Revelation* (Vol. 12, p. 197). Grand Rapids, MI: Zondervan Publishing House.

"Man, that is born of a woman is of few days, and full of trouble. He cometh forth like a flower and is cut down: he fleeth also as a shadow, and continueth not" (Job 14:1–2).[5]

Boasting in self-confidence is dangerous. To begin with, we know nothing about tomorrow; only God knows. The person who boasts about tomorrow is claiming to be God! Furthermore, life itself is uncertain—a cloud that quickly comes and goes.

Job 7:7, *"O remember that my life is wind: Mine eye shall no more see good."*

Psalm 102:3, *"For my days are consumed like smoke, And my bones are burned as an hearth."*

We do not even know when life will end, so how can we be so confident? We ought to say, *"If the Lord wills, we shall live …"* Every believer needs to keep before his or her eyes an awareness of the brevity of life. *"So, teach us to number our days, that we may apply our hearts unto wisdom"* (Psm 90:12).[6]

Boasting about an unknown future is sin. Yet so many people make plans without praying or seeking the mind of God. Pulled into the activities of the world, and seduced by its attractions, they live like the worldly-wise sinners who think they have security for the future but soon discover they have lost everything (cf Luke 12:15–21).[7]

In laying their plans with reference only to this world, these people have failed to reckon with a fundamental fact—the insubstantial and transitory nature of *"this world."* For such people as they are (a paraphrase of the indefinite relative *"hoitines,"* *"which temple ye are"*) to plan so confidently is the height of foolishness.[8]

---

5 Wiersbe, W. W. (1996). *The Bible exposition commentary* (Vol. 2, p. 371). Wheaton, IL: Victor Books.
6 Wiersbe, W. W. (1992). *Wiersbe's expository outlines on the New Testament* (p. 732). Wheaton, IL: Victor Books.
7 Wiersbe, W. W. (1992), 732.
8 Moo, D. J. (1985). (Vol. 16, p. 160).

Don't count on your time! It is passing! Don't count on your possessions! They will soon belong to someone else. Don't count on your profession! It will soon be over.[9]

Now I beseech you, brethren, by the name of our Lord Jesus Christ, that ye all speak the same thing, and that there be no divisions among you; but that ye be perfectly joined together in the same mind and in the same judgment" (I Cor 1:10).

"Fulfil ye my joy, that ye be like-minded, having the same love, being of one accord of one mind," (Philippians 2:2).

The whole idea of borrowing is an assumption that conditions will be better tomorrow than they are today. This outlook is condemned in James 4:13-17.

Whereas ye know not what shall be on the morrow...But now ye rejoice in your boastings: all such rejoicing is evil. Therefore, to him that knoweth to do good and doeth it not, to him it is sin.

The Financial Condition of a Church Reflects the Spiritual Condition of the Families Within the Church. When the church leaders have a vision of building the church, but a lack of funds hinders such a program, that should be God's signal to them to concentrate on the families. Thousands of churches, after having borrowed to build, often face tremendous financial pressures because of unexpected developments: families leaving, the pastor resigning, recession in the area, unexpected bills, *ad infinitum.*

Elsewhere the *Bible* depicts life.

- *"like a shadow that declineth"* (Psm 102:11); cf. Job 14:2).
- *"a whiff of breath"* (Job 7:7).
- *"A vanishing cloud"* (Job 7:9).
- *"A wild flower"* (Psalm 103:15).[10]

---

9 Ellsworth, R. (2009). *Opening up James* (p. 142). Leominster: Day One Publications.
10 Vaughan, C. (2003). *James* (p. 96). Cape Coral, FL: Founders Press.

Exodus 22:25 says, "*If thou lend money to any of My people that is poor by thee, thou shalt not be to him as an usurer, neither shalt thou lay upon him usury [interest].*"

See also Deuteronomy 23:19-20 and Leviticus 25:35-38.

Easton's Bible Dictionary explains these verses this way: "The Mosaic law required that when an Israelite needed to borrow, what he asked was to be freely lent to him, and no interest was to be charged, although interest might be taken from a foreigner. At the end of seven years all debts were remitted."

The *American Tract Society Dictionary* says, "Jehovah, as the sole proprietor of the land occupied by the Jews, required them, as one condition of it's very use, to grant liberal loans to their poor brethren, and every seven years, the outstanding loans were to become gifts, and could not be reclaimed."

Nehemiah rebuked the wealthy people of God in Israel who had refused to obey this admonition to be involved in the ministry of lending without charging interest. (See Neh 5:1–13).

The psalmist wrote in Psalm 112:5 that "*a good man sheweth favour, and lendeth: he will guide his affairs with discretion.*"

Paul wrote to Timothy that as a pastor he was to

Charge them that are rich in this world. That they do good, that they be rich in good works, ready to distribute, willing to communicate [participate in giving]. Laying up in store [heaven] for themselves a good foundation against the time to come (I Tim 6: 17-19).

In Luke 6:34-35 we hear Christ challenging believers who have been blessed with disposable income to "*do good...and lend.*"

II Corinthians 9:7 reminds us that this giving is to be done "*according as he [the lender] purposeth in his heart.*"

In summary, God owns everything, and we who are His subjects are stewards of what He has "loaned" us. He recognizes that we may not be able to give money that may be needed for the future, and thus He has given us the ministry of lending.

Chapter 6
The Ministry of Generosity

"There was a man, they called him mad; The more he gave, the more he had."[1] (cf. Matt 6:3)

Money Can't Buy Everything

Money has power. But it also has weaknesses. For instance, money can buy *land*, but not *love*; *bonds*, but not *brotherhood*; *gold*, but not *gladness*; *silver*, but not *sincerity*; *hospitals*, but not *health*; *condominiums*, but not *character*; *houses*, but not *homes*; *timber*, but not *truth*. Money can purchase *commodities*, but not *comfort*; *ranches*, but not *righteousness*; *ships*, but not *salvation*; and *hotels*, but not *heaven*. To *save* your money you must *share* it; to *love* it is to *lose* it; and to *invest* it forever, you must put it in things *eternal*.[2]

Give from Your Firstfruits

Proverbs 3:9-10 says, "*Honor the LORD with your wealth, with the first-fruits of all your crops; then your barns will be filled to overflowing, and your vats will brim over with new wine.*"

According to this verse, we honor God when we give to Him. To "*honor*" God means to "*give*" to Him. And we are to give from our "*wealth*." To give from your "crops" or from your "produce" means to give from your income. Giving from our income honors God or shows due respect, praise, and thanksgiving to Him for all that He has given us. When we fail to give to God, we dishonor Him.

---

1 Galaxie Software. (2002). *10,000 Sermon Illustrations*. Biblical Studies Press.
2 Hobbs, H. H. (1990). *My favorite illustrations* (p. 181). Broadman Press.

The next thing to note here is that we are to give God the "*firstfruits*" of our income. That means we are to give to Him "off the top." The "*firstfruits*" were the first crops gathered in at harvest time (Deut 26:1–11). They were the first in a series of more to come. This verse is telling us that every time we produce income, we need to honor God by first giving to Him from what He has given the power to produced. That means that when I cash it, the first thing I am going to do is give some money to God. The amount is not the issue—it's the priority of giving to God first that matters. That means with every source of income I receive; God becomes the priority in how I spend it. I will consider Him before any other thing, be it a bill I need to pay or a desired item I've been longing to buy.

This verse also says we are to give the firstfruits from "*all*" our income. If it's a check of $50 from a birthday card, a check of $500 from your weekly pay, or $5,000 from cashing in on your stock options. Giving as God increases is not to be restricted solely to monetary gains, but to everything we receive.

- Give *Graciously* from the value of presents.
- Give *Graciously* from an inheritance.
- Give *Graciously* from the increase you receive, over your purchase price, when you refinance a home to withdraw some equity, or when other property is sold.
- Give *Graciously* in "*all ways,*" and watch God's response.

He will not, He most certainly will not let you outgive Him, for He will be debtor to no man. Remember the widow's cruse of oil? "*And the barrel of meal wasted not, neither did the cruse of oil fail, according to the word of the Lord, which He spake by Elijah.*(I Kings 17:16). *Selah*!

When you exercise *Grace Giving*, people do not understand. They say, "You give far more than any of the rest of us, and yet you always seem to have more to give." Just keep shoveling, and watch God shovel back. And remember, God has the bigger shovel—Herbert Lockyer

God wants you to honor Him from ALL that He increases you. The beauty of this principle is that it is timeless, and it can apply to anyone on a practical level.

Proverbs 3:9-10, *"Honour the Lord with thy substance, And with the firstfruits of all thine increase: So shall thy barns be filled with plenty, And thy presses shall burst out with new wine."*

No matter how much or how often God gives you an increase—be it daily, weekly, monthly, annually, whenever—you can always fulfill this command of God by giving to Him from the firstfruits of your income.[3]

Big Interest

ONE afternoon a man got out of a street car to go to a home where his wife and he were to take tea with some friends. After paying his fare he had but seven cents left—all the money he had in the world. He did not even know where the money was coming from to buy breakfast for his family next morning, and yet he had no care as God had supplied needs so often, he knew that He would now. A young woman got on the car and went to the front end of the car and dropped her five cents in the box. The driver opened the door, shook his head, and said, "That five cents is bad." She said, "That is all the five cents I have." "Then," he said, "you must get off the car." The young woman was in great perplexity. The passenger thought of his seven cents in his pocket, all the money he had, but he went to the front end of the car and dropped five cents in the box and relieved the young woman's embarrassment. He felt no poorer. He had no doubt that before he needed money, money would come. As he was passing along the street a gentleman whom he knew, got out of a carriage, and went to his horse's head. He saw me passing and held out his hand and said, "How do you do? How are you getting on in your work?" He told him he was getting on nicely. "Well," he said, "I want to give something for your work," and he took out

---

[3] McManis, C. (2006). *Christian Living Beyond Belief: Biblical Principles for the Life of Faith* (pp. 110–111). Kress Christian Publications.

his pocketbook and gave him $200. The five cents had brought quick interest.[4]

Charles Spurgeon And His Wife according to a story in the *Chaplain* magazine, would sell, but refused to give away, the eggs their chickens laid. Even close relatives were told, "You may have them if you pay for them." As a result, some people labeled the Spurgeons greedy and grasping. They accepted the criticisms without defending themselves, and only after Mrs. Spurgeon died was the full story revealed. All the profits from the sale of eggs went to support two elderly widows. Because the Spurgeons where unwilling to let their left hand know what the right hand was doing (Matt. 6:3), they endured the attacks in silence[5]

George Muller -- If we could look behind the unexpected events in our lives, we would be amazed to see God wonderfully providing for our needs. The apparent insignificant turns in the road, the seemingly inconsequential events, the often-inexplicable occurrences—all are part of God's loving care. His gracious providence is also evident in the tangible provisions of life.

In Bristol, England, George Muller operated an orphanage for over two thousand children. One evening he became aware that there would be no breakfast for them the next morning. Muller called his workers together and explained the situation. Two or three prayed. "Now that is sufficient," he said. "Let us rise and praise God for prayer answered!" The next morning, they could not push open the great front door. So, they went out the back door and around the building to see what was keeping it shut. Stacked up against the front door were boxes filled with food. One of the workers later remarked, "We know Who sent the baskets, but we do not know who brought them!"[6]

---

4 Torrey, R. A. (1907). *Anecdotes and illustrations* (pp. 55–57). Fleming H. Revell Co.
5 Galaxie Software. (2002).
6 Galaxie Software. (2002). *Our Daily Bread*, November 30, 1993

Three Levels of Giving

1. You have to—(Law)

2. You ought to—(Obligation)

3. You want to—(Grace) ~ Waldo Weaning[7]

Christian giving is always a response. The motivation for our giving is that we have received from the Lord. This doesn't mean we try to pay God back, for that is an impossibility. It does mean that our giving begins in gratitude.[8] I shovel out and God shovels in, and He uses a bigger shovel than I do. And remember God started the shoveling first.[9] Remember Calvary?

---

7 Galaxie Software. (2002).
8 Jones, G. C. (1986). *1000 illustrations for preaching and teaching.* Nashville, TN: Broadman & Holman Publishers.
9 Jones, G. C. (1986). (p. 331).

CHAPTER 7

EATING AN ELEPHANT ONE BITE AT A TIME[1]

The African Elephant is the largest living land animal. When full grown, males will be 10-12 feet tall at the shoulder, and weigh between 10,000 and 12,000 pounds. To withstand blistering sun and torrential rains, the skin of an elephant can be up to 1.5 inches thick. Its diet consists of vegetation in the form of grasses, tree limbs, tubers (roots), fruits, vines, and shrubs. Elephants will spend up to 16 hours each day foraging for the 300+ pounds of vegetation they must consume to meet their daily nutritional needs. By focusing on his enormous daily need, the elephant assures the requirements of his future are being attended.

"A JOURNEY OF A THOUSAND MILES BEGINS WITH A SINGLE STEP"—LAO TZU.

By focusing NOT on what you must achieve over the course of the next year, but instead on what you are doing now, each moment, each hour, each day, you are facing something achievable. **Over time, that small change will add up to a huge transformation,** and you will be surprised at how far you come in no time.

As with the voracious appetite of a 12,000-pound elephant, the "behemoth" of finances has caused nations to go to war, brought down kings and kingdoms, bankrupt both secular businesses and churches, and is the source of the ruination of far too many marriages. Be it governments, kingdoms, or individuals—the challenges of finances,

---

[1] The proverb became popular in the 1940s and 1950s, when it was accepted to have been of Chinese origin.

while astonishing and shocking, are manageable. The handling of finances requires both an assessment of our actions, and application of absolute self-discipline.

Pastor Warren Wiersbe wrote, "God's people today don't offer animals to the Lord as in *Old Testament* times, because Jesus Christ has fulfilled the Law and fulfilled all the sacrifices in His death on the cross (Heb 10:1–14). But as the priests of God, believers today offer up spiritual sacrifices through Him: our bodies (Rom 12:1–2); people won to the Saviour (Rom 15:16); money (Phil 4:18); praise and good works (Heb 13:15–16); a broken heart (Psm 51:17); and our prayers of faith (Psm 141:1–2). Yes, it is good to have the things that money can buy, provided you don't lose the things that money can't buy."[2]

In Ecclesiastes 5:10-17, Solomon, the wealthiest man of his day (I Kings 10:23), and the wisest man who ever lived, gave at least five principles concerning wealth and greed:

1. **The More Wealth One Has, The More He *Wants*:** *"He that loveth silver shall not be satisfied with silver; nor he that loveth abundance with increase: this is also vanity"* (v. 10).

2. **The More Wealth One Has, The More He *Spends*:** *"When goods increase, they are increased that eat them"* (v. 11).

3. **The More Wealth One Has, The More He *Worries*:** *"…but the abundance of the rich will not suffer him to sleep"* (v. 12).

4. **The More Wealth One Has The More Potential He Has To Lose:** *"…but those riches perish by evil travail"* (vv. 13-14).

5. **The More Wealth One Has, The More He Will *Leave* Behind:** *"As he came forth of his mother's womb, naked shall he return to go as he came, and shall take nothing of his labour, which he may carry away in his hand"* (vv. 15-17).

---

2 Wiersbe, W. W. (1996). *Be Satisfied* (p. 69). Victor Books.

"A JOURNEY OF A THOUSAND MILES BEGINS WITH A SINGLE STEP"—LAO TZU.

A. **Wealth and God**

Solomon also gave two divine perspectives concerning the Lord and wealth:

1). **The Results Of A Man's Labor** (i.e., his wealth and possessions).

   Ecclesiastes 6:2, *"A man to whom God hath given riches, wealth, and honour, so that he wanteth nothing for his soul of all that he desireth, yet God giveth him not power to eat thereof, but a stranger eateth it: this is vanity, and it is an evil disease."*

   And the ability to enjoy them and to be happy (cf. 8:15) in his work, are gifts of God (cf. 2:24; 3:13).[3]

   "Every man also to whom God hath given riches and wealth, and hath given him power to eat thereof" (**v. 19**).

2). This ability to enjoy life, this gladness of heart with which God occupies those thus gifted, keeps a person from brooding over life's brevity (days of his life in 5:20 refers back to *"few days"* in **v. 18**).[4]

GOD GIVES MAN THE ABILITY TO ENJOY HIS WEALTH.

".... because God answereth him in the joy of his heart" (**v. 20**).

---

3 Glenn, D. R. (1985). *Ecclesiastes*. In J. F. Walvoord & R. B. Zuck (Eds.), *The Bible Knowledge Commentary: An Exposition of the Scriptures* (Vol. 1, pp. 989–990). Victor Books.
4 Glenn, D. R., (Vol. 1, p. 990).

B. Wealth and Giving

The *Bible* in general, and the *NT* specifically, teach basic truths about one's wealth that honors the Lord Jesus Christ.

1). In The *Old Testament,* The Tithe Was God's Amount:

"Bring ye all the tithes into the storehouse, that there may be meat in Mine house, and prove Me now herewith, saith the LORD of hosts, if I will not open you the windows of heaven, and pour you out a blessing, that there shall not be room enough to receive it" (Mal 3:10).

2). The Institution of the Local *New Testament* Church Is God's Agency For the Care of the Saints:

"Now concerning the collection for the saints, as I have given order to the churches of Galatia, even so do ye. Upon the first day of the week let every one of you lay by him in store, as God hath prospered him, that there be no gatherings when I come" (I Cor 16:1-2).

3). The Purpose Of Giving Is To Accomplish The Great Commission:

"Go ye therefore, and teach all nations, baptizing them in the name of the Father, and of the Son, and of the Holy Ghost: Teaching them to observe all things whatsoever I have commanded you: and, lo, I am with you alway, even unto the end of the world. Amen" (Matt 28:19-20).

4). The Secret Of Giving Is To First Give One's Heart:

"And this they did, not as we hoped, but first gave their own selves to the Lord, and unto us by the will of God" (II Cor. 8:5).

5). The Eternal State Is The Final Investment:

"And I say unto you, Make to yourselves friends of the mammon of unrighteousness; that, when ye fail, they may receive you into everlasting habitations" (Luke 16:9).

Conclusion:

For the Christian to succumb to the temptation of *"the love of money"* (I Tim 6:10) is vanity indeed. The only institution that has the divine guarantee of perpetuity is the Lord's local *NT* church (Matt 28:19-20).

In other things believers everywhere zealously declare the *Bible* to be their only rule of faith and practice; but in the matter of giving have adopted a great deal of latitude. In the giving of money for the carrying on of His worship and work, they consider their personal convenience, resort to their particular campaigns, adopting their peculiar criteria. Selecting their way of doing things, they have not quite thought to inquire whether their Lord and Master had given them any directions on the subject.

The *Bible* has been left out, and all sorts of human choices adopted to raise money (Bake sales, potluck dinners with donations of course, Annual Faith Promise Missions commitments, building fund appeals, and endless pleas to support "special collections").

We have chosen our own way and have not hearkened to the law of the Lord.[5] Five hundred years from now, if the Lord has not yet returned, will this enormously erroneous economic tradition still be in play? Will the Lord's people still be attempting to finance the Lord's churches through *OT* debt rules of tithes and offerings? Or will we have the **Peace**, the **Provision** and the **Pleasure** of **Practicing** Grace Giving. *Selah!*

---

5 Charles A. Cook, Stewardship and Missions, pp. 92-93.

Chapter 8
THE MINISTRY OF EXTREME LIVING
(Colossians 1:1-14)

"GOD DOES NOT EXPECT US TO IMITATE JESUS CHRIST: HE EXPECTS US TO ALLOW THE LIFE OF JESUS CHRIST TO BE MANIFESTED IN [US]."

In this century, a favorite buzzword is "*Extreme*." High intensity pastimes such as bungee jumping, rock climbing, mountain bike races, skateboarding, skydiving, snowboarding, and much more are commonplace activities. Our minds are flooded by the internet (Facebook, Google, Twitter, TikTok and such). Our senses are anesthetized by appalling television programs, driving our wicked hearts into the darkness, and further annihilating spiritual truths.

The irony is that in the midst of such physical extremity, far too many Christians embrace intellectual dishonesty, encourage confrontational violence, and engage in spiritual absurdity and vulgarity. This Woke, Me-Too, If-It-Feels-Good-Do-It generation calls for tolerance, moderation, and for what it consider is politically correct (PC); insisting on intellectual "self-determination." "Have it your way," in matters of the body, the mind, and the spirit. Chaos reigns, human degradation abounds, and the "Tower of Babel" mentality accelerates the just deployment of God's wrath.

In an age that values intense, extreme experiences, we need to exhibit an intense, **Extreme Faith**. And when we talk about intensity, when we talk about high-octane, high adrenaline, extreme faith. Nobody did it better than the Moravians.

The Moravians officially established their community in 1457, sixty years before Luther nailed his *95 Theses* on the door of the Wittenberg church. For 250 years, the Moravians suffered intense persecution for their beliefs, until 1722 when Count Ludwig von Zinzendorf, a man of deep-rooted faith, invited them to sanctuary on his estate. The refugees picked up from Czechoslovakia and Bohemia and came to the refugee village in Germany called "Herrnhut," meaning *"the Lord's Watch."*

Other religious refugees also came—French Calvinists and German Anabaptists among them. In time, the blending of nationalities and ideas brought about conflict. Zinzendorf, the *de facto* leader of this group, was disturbed by the tension, and had been praying about it with key community leaders.

On August 13, 1727, their prayers were answered. The community had assembled for a communion service, and in that service, the entire body felt the presence of the Holy Spirit leading them to beg forgiveness of one another, and to seek reconciliation. This service was described as a "Second Pentecost." It was a **Rebirth**, a **Renewal**, a God sent **Revival**.

Something happened to the Moravians during that service—they were transformed from being a dissimilar group of refugees into an enthusiastic band of disciples, ready for any task. After August 13, 1727, the Moravians moved from **Extreme Persecution** to **Extreme Faith.**

First, they began with **Extreme Prayer**. Giving continual thanks to God was characteristic of Paul's prayers:

> *We give thanks to God and the Father of our Lord Jesus Christ, praying always for you"* (Col 1:3).
>
> *"For this cause we also, since the day we heard it, do not cease to pray for you, and to desire that ye might be filled with the knowledge of his will in all wisdom and spiritual understanding"* (Col 1:9).

Shortly after that monumental communion service, the Moravians began the practice of "**Hourly Intercession**." This was a prayer vigil consisting of a rotating assignment of one man and one woman from the Moravian community praying every hour of the day.

How long do you think they were able to keep up this continual rotation of prayer? A week? A month? How about over 100 years. Over 100 years of non-stop prayer. Not only is that extreme, but it shatters our understanding of the definition of extreme.

A friend of mine told me he rises at 4:30 each morning and falls on his knees by his bedside to begin his day in prayer. There **IS** something extreme about rising at 4:30 in the morning, every morning, to be part of a prayer rotation. But even so, none have touched the 100-year record held by the Moravians in Herrnhut.

- Can you **Picture** the **Unity** that came from such a practice?
- Can you **Imagine** the **Personal Growth** experienced by those praying people?
- Can you **Fathom** the **Spiritual Power** unleashed by such non-stop intercession?

II Corinthians 5:14 ~ "*For the love of Christ constraineth us....*"

The thing that hinders God's work is not gross sin, but other claims (duties) which **ARE Right**, but which at a certain point of their 'rightness' conflict with the claims of Christ. If the conflict should come, remember that it is to be Jesus first. (Oswald Chambers).

> "*If any man come to Me, and hate not his father, and mother, and wife, and children, and brethren, and sisters, yea, and his own life also, he cannot be My disciple*" (Luke 14:26).

The emphasis here is on the ***Priority Of Love*** (Matt 10:37). "*He that loveth father or mother more than Me is not worthy of Me: and he that loveth son or daughter more than Me is not worthy of Me.*"

One's loyalty to Jesus must come before loyalty to his family, or even to life itself. Indeed, those who did follow Jesus against their families' desires were thought of as hating their families.[1] Missionary Henry Martyn said about God—"I shall never have to regret that I have loved Thee too well."

What was unleashed from that **Extreme Praying** was ~ **Extreme Witness.** Colossians 1:4-5 summarize the eternal hope we have through Jesus Christ—the compelling hope of everlasting life, not earned by our good works, but graciously given by a loving father. *"Since we heard of your faith in Christ Jesus, and of the love which ye have to all the saints, For the hope, which is laid up for you in heaven, whereof ye heard before in the word of the truth of the gospel."*

Then in verse 6, Paul tells us that this good news, this Gospel, is bearing fruit all over the world. *"Which is come unto you, as it is in all the world; and bringeth forth fruit, as it doth also in you, since the day ye heard of it, and knew the grace of God in truth:"*

Paul is being modest. He is the primary catalyst for that fruit. He traveled all over the Mediterranean planting churches. Paul was **Extreme** in his **Witness.**

In the same **Extreme Way**, the Moravians took their proclamation of the Gospel around the world.

Supported by the spiritual power of the hourly intercessions, Moravian missionaries began to venture forth from Herrnhut. In 1732, they sent their first two missionaries to the West Indies. John Leonard Dober and David Nitschman—unsung heroes. These men were not going on an enjoyable short-term missions trip to the Caribbean, or Africa or China, but they sold themselves into slavery to answer the call "come and minister the Gospel to us."

To circumvent the restrictions imposed by foreign merchants in the West Indies, the men became slaves in order to have the opportunity to

---

1 Walvoord, J. F., Zuck, R. B., & Dallas Theological Seminary, (1985). *The Bible Knowledge Commentary: An Exposition of the Scriptures* (Luke 14:25–27). Wheaton, IL: Victor Books.

reach the slaves of the West Indies for the Lord. Their life's resolve was to follow the Lamb, who had given His life for them, and for all the souls of the world. Their mission statement was "Our Lamb has conquered, let us follow Him." It gives new meaning to the phrase "sold out for Christ."

- In 1733, a group of Moravians established a colony in Greenland.
- In 1734 a band of 18, was sent to set up a colony on the island of St. Croix. Within a year, 10 of those missionaries died. Herrnhut sent 11 more volunteers, and 9 more died.

Powered by the unceasing intercession, the tiny village of Herrnhut **EXPLODED**, and sent missionaries around the world proclaiming the good news of Jesus Christ.

By 1737, just four years later, the Moravians were in South Africa. Jamaica, Barbados, Guyana, North Carolina, Georgia, Pennsylvania, London, East Africa, Alaska, Canada, Honduras, Nicaragua, California, Australia, Tibet, and Jerusalem.

Their *Extreme Prayer* **POWERED** their *Extreme Witness,* which was **VALIDATED** by their *Extreme Lifestyle*.

Acknowledge Him in all your ways, and He will bring you into circumstances that will develop the particular side of your life that He wants developed and be careful that you do not upset His plans by bringing in your own ideas ~ Oswald Chambers.

Look at verses 10-13 of our passage.

*That ye might walk **worthy** of the Lord unto all pleasing, being **fruitful** in every good work, and **increasing** in the knowledge of God; **Strengthened** with all might, according to His glorious power, unto all **Patience** and **Longsuffering** with **Joyfulness**; Giving thanks unto the Father, Which hath made us meet to be partakers of the inheritance of the saints in light: Who hath* *delivered us from the power of darkness, and hath translated us into the kingdom of His dear Son.*

Paul's **Prayer** is that his readers would lead a lifestyle worthy of the Lord—bearing fruit in every good work.

Paul's **Position** is that all of life is worship—We don't just play some religious game on Sundays. Rather, everything we do, whether at work or play, whether with family, friends or alone—**EVERYTHING WE DO**, we do for the glory of God.

The Moravians made this attitude a "**Trademark Of Their Witness.**" Wherever they went they established colonies. In these colonies, all the single men lived together, all the single women lived together, and they shared resources.

When they set up these colonies, they didn't just send Preachers—they sent Craftsmen. They sent people who were good at their trades, so they could sustain the colony, and bring glory to God through their excellence skills.

- Their belief was that the life of the community was an expression of praise and glory to God.

- Every moment, every breath, was an opportunity to live for God.

The Moravians were examples of Paul's attitude of *Extreme Faith*: *Extreme Prayer, Extreme Witness,* and *Extreme Lifestyle.*

Their living example of faith in Jesus Christ had a broader impact than most people know.

- In the 18th century, a young Baptist Preacher in London read about the missionary feats of the Moravians and stormed into the Baptist convention saying, "Look at what these Moravians have done! Cannot we follow their example and in obedience to our Heavenly Master go out into the world, and preach the Gospel to the heathen?" His name ~ William Carey, and he became the first Baptist missionary.

- On a perilous sea voyage from London to the British colony of Georgia, two young Anglican preachers found themselves confined on a small ship in a massive storm. They, along with the rest of the passengers and the crew, feared for their lives. There was only one exception to the panic on board—a band of Moravians who spent the entire storm singing hymns and praising God. The two Anglican preachers were so impressed by the faith of the Moravians that they sought them out and spent time with them. When the two returned to London, they began to worship with the Moravian community. One night at a service on Aldersgate Street, one of those young men experienced what he called a "warming of the heart." His name was John Wesley.

People heard the stories of the Moravians, they encountered them, and were inspired with their passion and fire.

Our LORD has a bold calling **For Us, For Me, For You, For Each One Of Us.**

Does the story of the Moravians inspire you?

WHAT WILL YOU DO WITH IT?

- ✓ Will you **Live** a bit more **Adventurously**?
- ✓ Will you **Proclaim** your faith a bit more **Aggressively**?
- ✓ Will you **Contemplate** Christ's claim on your life a bit more **Assertively**?
- ✓ Will you **Give Of Yourself** and your possessions in some new and **Astonishing** way?

In these days, we are called upon to be *Extreme In Our Lifestyle*.

In these days, we are called upon to be *Extreme In Our Prayers*.

In these days, we are called upon to be *Extreme In Our Faith*.

In these days, we are called upon to be *Extreme In Our Witness*.

Oswald Chambers said, "All God's men are ordinary men made extraordinary by the *(being obedient to that)* matter God has given them."

ABOUT THE AUTHOR

Dr. Ray Borah earned his Bachelor of Arts degree in Bible, History and English in 1973 from Bob Jones University, a Master of Science degree in Business and Computer Science from Abilene Christian University at Dallas, TX in 1985. He earned a Master of Religious Education degree from Tabernacle Baptist Theological Seminary in 1996 and earned his Doctorate in 1998 from the same institution.

Dr Borah retired as an Intelligence Specialist Chief Petty Officer from the US Navy in January 1998 and arrived on the mission field in the West Indies in August 1998. During his Christian life, he has served as youth pastor, assistant pastor, Christian school administrator/principal, Bible teacher, pastor, and missionary. Dr Borah flew aircraft in support of missionaries for 30 years. He also helped in starting, and served for over seven years as Registrar, at Calvary Baptist Bible College in Carolina, Puerto Rico and for over 8 years as the Academic Dean of North Love Baptist Bible College in Rockford, IL.

Dr Borah and his wife Sharon have 9 children, 35 grandchildren and 45 great-grandchildren.

Printed in the USA
CPSIA information can be obtained
at www.ICGtesting.com
JSHW052109071023
49651JS00011B/19

9 781630 734442